# Starting the School Year Well

AND

# What to Do If Things Go Awry

## An Autistic Student-Centered Approach to All-Year Success

I0814718

Brenda Smith Myles, PhD & Diane Adreon, EdD

**Starting the School Year Well and What to Do If Things Go Awry**
**An Autistic Student-Centered Approach to All-Year Success**

All marketing and publishing rights guaranteed to and reserved by:

**FUTURE HORIZONS**

(817) 277-0727
www.fhautism.com



ISBN: 978-1-963367-20-1

# Contents

# Contents

# PART I

# The Same Thing Happens Every Year

Most students thrive with consistency. Consistency is especially important for autistic students. Without consistency in their daily lives, we can expect autistic students to experience higher levels of anxiety and, consequently, more meltdowns. At school, this usually results in lost instructional time. **Because of their neurology, autistic students learn best when they know (a) what they are going to do, (b) when they are going to do it, and (c) with whom they will do it.**

Yet, despite our knowledge about autistic neurology and well-intended efforts, we regularly create a lack of predictability for students when they transition from year to year. It's not that we don't try to create consistency. We've read last year's individualized education program (IEP), participated in creating a new one, and read all the information in the student's file. Last year's teacher has even passed on "the box." "The box" typically contains *some* of the supports the student used during the previous year. (*Some* is emphasized here because the teacher may have kept one or two for future use with other students. In addition, "the box" generally includes no directions regarding how and when to use the supports.)

**So, what do you do?** As any good educational professional would, you engage in informal assessment and start out with trial and error. You seek to determine (a) what the student knows, (b) how they learn, and (c) what supports best assist the student throughout the day. While this is happening, the student may be learning, but not well.

After two to three months, you have gotten to know the student well and made adjustments here and there, and finally, learning occurs as the needed structure and supports are put into use. The year progresses with adjustments throughout—as is to be expected. Then year ends. And the process starts again for the student and their new teacher.

**Our students can miss up to five years of instructional time!** All because we do not have a consistent method to help them move seamlessly from grade to grade (Henry and Myles 2024).

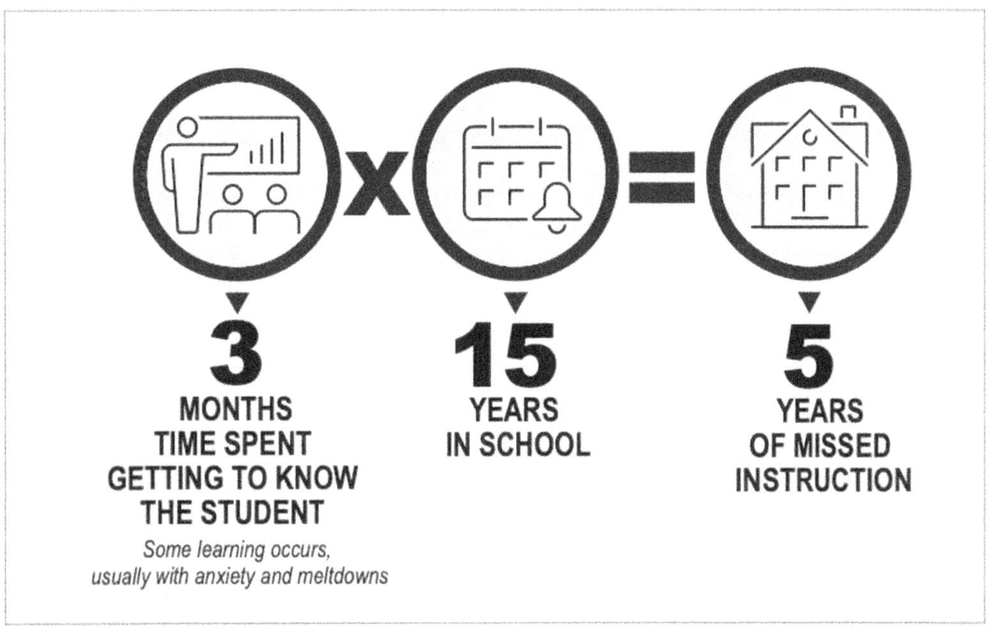


This book rectifies this issue by providing a comprehensive yet easy-to-use package to help transition students from year to year. Completion of these instruments creates a smoother transition that allows instructional time to be optimized and, as a result, intensifies learning.

And ... just in case the student experiences challenges, we have also included information that may be helpful. In some instances, it is necessary to revisit and modify the plan we have for students. When a student experiences distress that disrupts their learning and social interactions, we need to ask ourselves, "What do we need to do to help this student do better?" In this circumstance, this book will be helpful.

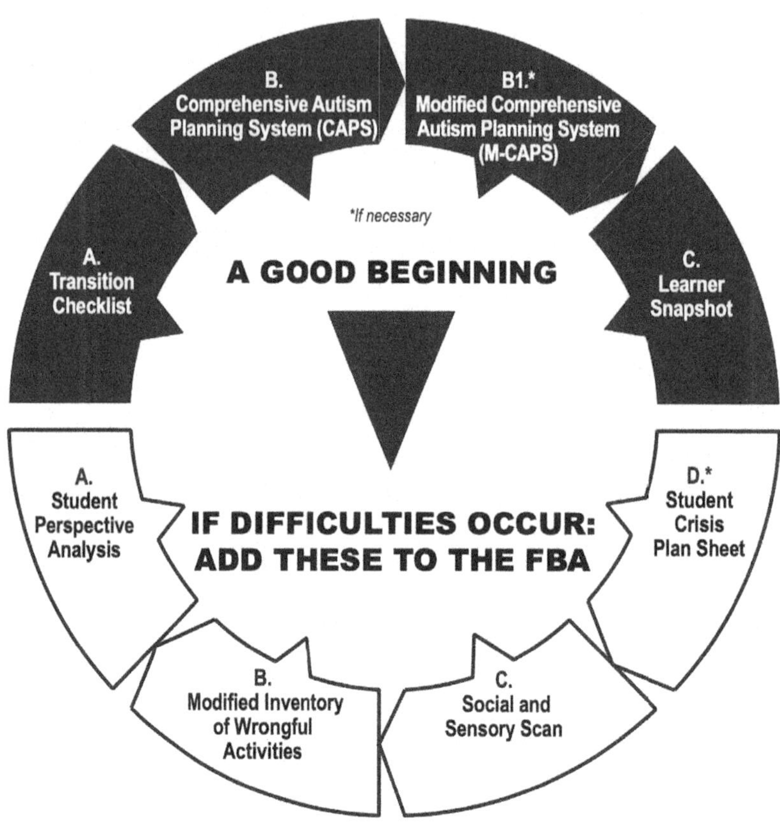


To pull everything together, the final chapter of the book consists of a case study that illustrates how this comprehensive package can help students not only survive but thrive at school.

Before we get started, it is important to define the following terms that will be used throughout the book.

| Terms and Definitions | |
|---|---|
| **School team members** | General educator, special educator, parent, school administrator, speech-language pathologist, occupational therapist, psychologist, paraprofessional, counselor, and relevant others |
| **Sending team** | School team members who support the autistic student *before* they transition |
| **Receiving team** | School team members who support the autistic student *after* they transition |

# PART II

# A Good Beginning

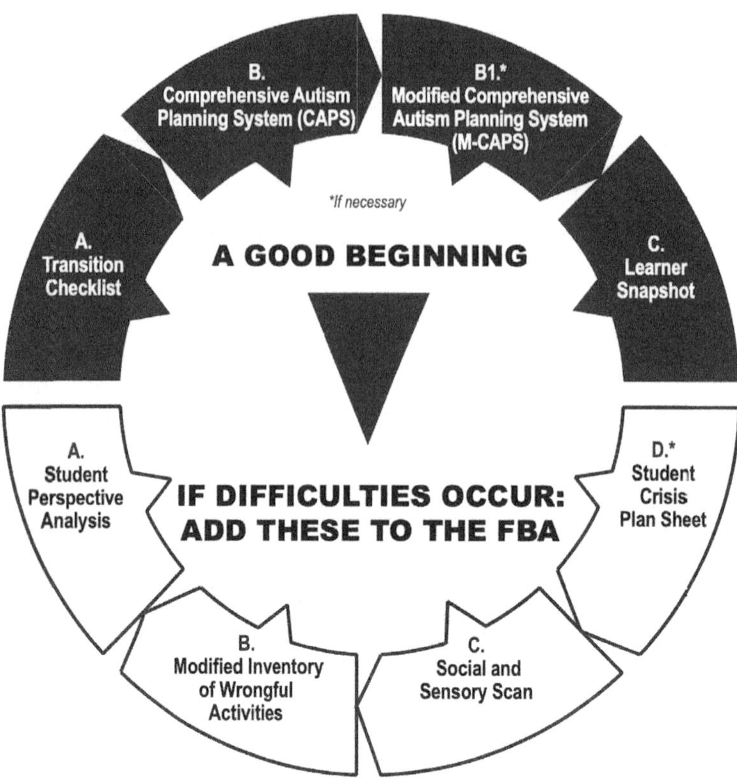


Part II of this book introduces the following instruments that, when used together, create a successful transition to the new school year:

- **Transition Checklist (K-12).** Using this instrument, the sending team lists the supports needed for student success in these areas: environmental supports, social supports, and academic modifications. The section called "Preplanning" indicates what the receiving team needs to do to prepare the student for the transition to a new grade. Each support is described with examples.

- **Comprehensive Autism Planning System (CAPS) (K-12).** The CAPS, also called the *practical individualized education program* (IEP), is completed by the receiving team when they create the student's IEP. The information provided enables everyone in the student's environment to know *what* supports are needed and *when* they are needed (Henry and Myles 2024).

- **Learner Snapshot (K-12).** This document, completed by parents, and sometimes the student themselves, describes (a) demographic information; (b) how the student learns best; (c) special interests, motivators, and preferences; (d) strengths and challenges; (e) issues related to being upset and having meltdowns; and (f) general modifications and accommodations. This form is particularly important for the student who is transitioning to a new school.

# Chapter 1

## Transition Checklist

*Amy Moore Gaffney, MA, CCC-SLP, and Brenda Smith Myles, PhD*

Transitions are difficult for most students, but they are more stressful and have more negative long-lasting effects on the autistic student than their neuromajority peers. Most neuromajority students need some support, at least temporarily, to transition successfully from one grade to the next. For example, they may have to be reminded to carry their new schedule with them for the first week or arrive at their locker in time to gather materials before class. The situation is different for many autistic students. Because of neurological challenges related to regulation, prediction, context, sensory issues, and learning, autistic students are likely to need significantly more supports during transitions from year to year (Fontil et al. 2020; Nuske et al. 2019).

Transition must not be thought of as a one-shot deal. Instead, it should be viewed as an ongoing process that addresses the changing academic, social, emotional, and physical needs of the student. To make the experience as positive as possible, parents and teachers must be proactive in transition planning.

Before the school year begins, transition planning must identify all the supports the student needs and ensure they are ready to be implemented on day one. To ensure the best possible outcomes for autistic individuals during otherwise challenging yearly transitions, this chapter takes a step-by-step look at the components of effective transition planning using the Transition Checklist.

This comprehensive checklist helps ensure that all steps are in place for a smooth transition. Simply put: The student's sending team completes the Transition Checklist (see example at the end of the chapter) at the end of the school year and forwards it to the student's new or receiving team. Thus, it allows the receiving team to take advantage of what was learned about the student during the prior year.

Dhia was transitioning to sixth grade in the fall. In April, Dhia's educational team, including parents—the sending team—completed the Transition Checklist along with her IEP. These documents were then shared with the receiving sixth-grade team so they could develop a successful transition plan for Dhia.

## Description

A discussion of the elements of the Transition Checklist follows.

### Preplanning

#### *Conducting or Reviewing Assessments:*

Meaningful assessment records can serve as initial guides to the transition planning process. This includes (a) diagnostic assessment if this has not been previously completed; (b) curriculum-based assessment of academic strengths and concerns; (c) formal and informal measures of sensory, social, and language skills; and (d) functional assessment of behaviors and perceptions. These assessments provide the groundwork for an appropriate education for the autistic student.

#### *Choosing Next Environment:*

Depending on the community in which the student lives, the size of the school district, and other family and community factors, several placement options are usually available and should be considered as future programming is planned. It is strongly recommended that possible environments be carefully analyzed early in the year prior to the transition to secure the best possible placement and avoid unnecessary challenges.

When selecting a program, families and school personnel should take into serious consideration the impressions and opinions of the student to ensure that they buy into the program and, therefore, will be more likely to do well. If possible, it is important to help the student see a range of options, including public, charter, magnet, and private schools, as well as homeschooling.

#### *Transition Planning Meeting:*

Once the school has been selected, the next step in ensuring a successful transition is to hold a transition planning meeting. Whenever possible, it is important that the sending *and* receiving teams attend to ensure continuing communication and support.

During the meeting, all participants should focus on identifying supports the student needs to survive the first weeks of school and determining how to implement them. It is also important to set up a schedule for future meetings and any training that is deemed necessary. As discussed below, sound transition planning includes teacher training as well as student orientation. Depending on the student's needs and the nature of the program being transitioned into, the planning meeting may need to be scheduled as early as the spring before the transition in order to allow sufficient planning time. The agenda is included in the Transition Checklist (see end of this chapter).

### *Training for School Personnel:*

When selecting the best class/school for the student, a major consideration is to ensure that the receiving team understands autism and how it impacts the student. Even if this condition has been satisfied initially, it may still be necessary to check that staff understand how to implement the various supports that are needed for a given student's success. If additional training is deemed necessary, it should occur before the start of the new school year and before the student's orientation so teachers are familiar with the student's strengths, interests, and needs before meeting them for the first time. Guidelines for staff training and orientation appear in the Transition Checklist (see end of this chapter).

### *Student Orientation:*

Getting used to new situations is always easier and less threatening given proper advance notice and preparation. Nowhere is this truer than for the autistic student who is transitioning to a new grade, as the student's need for routine, sameness, and predictability is severely challenged during times of change.

To reduce the student's anxiety upon entering a new class or school, a sound orientation program conducted well in advance of the actual transition is essential. Such orientation should include familiarization with the physical setting of the class and school as needed, introduction to all pertinent teachers and staff, and explanation of rules for behavior as well as academic performance. Familiarizing the student with procedures, such as getting lunch and waiting for the bus, should also occur. Other helpful aspects of student orientation include meeting peer "buddies"; sharing names and possibly photos of teachers, administrators, and trusted support person; and so on.

### *Environmental Supports:*

To enhance school success for autistic students, we often must modify or enhance the environment to meet individual strengths and needs. In addition to being taught how to use specific supports, the student must learn to recognize when they need the support as well as how to request it. Environmental supports include (a) preferential seating, (b) organizational strategies, (c) home base, (d) trusted support person, (e) personal visual supports, and (f) classroom visual supports, as described below.

### *Preferential Seating:*

Care should be taken when assigning desks. Make sure the autistic student's desk is placed so that the teacher can easily monitor the student's attention to task without calling undue notice. Also, do not place the student near high-traffic areas (close to the waste basket or pencil sharpener) or near windows that provide opportunities for distraction. Sona Chadwick (personal communication 2000) recommends placing carefully selected peers at least two deep in all directions from the autistic student. These peers can be helpful to the autistic individual who might need a small prompt to turn to the right page in a textbook, for example. Finally, the student's desk should be facing the teacher—this helps with orientation and reduces the fatigue related to frequent movement.

### *Organizational Strategies:*

Organizational challenges frequently mask the academic competence of autistic students (Cavalli 2022; Pasqualotto 2021). For example, it is fairly common for autistic students to complete homework assignments but fail to turn them in. Often this is because they cannot find them in their crowded, disheveled backpack. At other times, they may find the assignment but do not know where and when to turn it in.

Organization also requires knowing what papers to keep and what papers can be discarded. Autistic students tend to keep all papers because of their difficulty in determining the status of each and, thus, require instruction, supports, multiple practice opportunities, and coaching to develop and use organization skills. Other organizational skills needed in school include how to open a locker and locate needed supplies for each class.

Time management is often a challenge too. Because autistic students frequently have "time blindness," that is, an inability to estimate how long it will take to complete an assignment (Hus 2022), they may plan to read a book about planets and write a five-page essay on the importance of the Constitution all on Sunday evening, even though the essay is due on Monday. Other students have trouble initiating a book report or science project because they do not have the skills to break down the tasks into smaller components.

Learning how to develop timelines is an important organizational skill. Timelines help students understand the various tasks that need to be completed and provide guidance regarding reasonable time frames to complete each step. The importance of organizational strategies for autistic individuals and samples of organizational supports may be found at https://learningforapurpose.com/how-to-help-teens-with-autism-with-organization-skills/.

### *Home Base:*

A *home base* is a quiet place in the school where students can go to (a) plan or review information or (b) cope with stress and behavioral challenges (Kreibich et al. 2020). It also serves as a place the student can go if (a) the classroom is becoming overwhelming, (b) a teacher thinks a meltdown may be on the way, or (c) the student otherwise needs a place to calm. There are no specific criteria for the location or other characteristics of a home base.

Home base is not a time-out, nor is it somewhere a student goes to escape work. Primarily, it should be a positive place for the student, located anywhere that is quiet and comfortable, such as a resource room, a favorite teacher's classroom, or an ancillary staff member's office.

Use of home base is individually determined. Some students primarily use it to deal with stress and behavioral challenges, whereas others use it on a regular basis to plan and review information. Time at home base can be scheduled into a student's school day and may be especially helpful if scheduled immediately following a class period or activity that proves stressful for the autistic student. A hall pass is often used to prompt the student to take a break. Additional information about home base may be found at https://autisminternetmodules.org/m/1033.

### *Trusted Support Person:*

A *trusted support person* is an adult in whom the autistic is comfortable confiding and being around. It is ideal if this person supervises home base. The role of this person can be multifaceted. In addition to supporting the student in home base, they can (a) teach social skills, (b) interpret social situations, (c) listen and empathize, or (d) help the student achieve emotional "readiness" for upcoming activities.

The specific role depends on student need, the amount of time available for support, and the adult's qualifications. For example, if the student has developed rapport with the head custodian and wants to talk over social issues with him, that might be an option. The custodian would not be in charge of providing instruction, but with time and training, the custodian could help the autistic student better understand social situations (see "Social Skills Interpretation" in this chapter). On the other hand, if the resource room teacher serves as the trusted support person, they can provide a full complement of social and sensory instruction.

### *Personal Visual Supports:*

Many students require individualized supports to ensure that they understand their environment and work responsibilities. Personal visual supports allow the student to navigate their day successfully. Such supports may include the following:

- A map of the school that depicts classes and routes to get to them; when to go to the locker (if in middle or high school); and important locations, such as the bathroom, auditorium, principal's office, and so forth.

- A list of class locations, room numbers, and supplies needed posted inside notebooks and locker, if appropriate. This may also be included on the visual schedule.

- List of teacher expectations and classroom routines. These can be placed inside the student's notebook for each class or be a part of the student's mini-schedule.

- The classroom visual schedule showing the student's academic and nonacademic classes, such as music class, lunch, recess, science, or geometry. Even though it is posted in the classroom, the student may need to keep a personal copy of this schedule with them during the school day.

- A mini-schedule that lists specifically what will occur during a class in the appropriate order, such as group work, test, silent reading, lecture, game. The learner needs one mini-schedule for each class.

- A symbol, such as a lightning bolt or asterisk, that communicates that a change in the schedule will occur.

- Test reminders to remove the element of surprise. It is necessary to determine how many days before the test the reminder will be shared, what the reminder will look like, and how to ensure that the student understands the reminder and can successfully prepare for the test.

- Hall pass and hall pass routine that allow the student to access home base, locker, bathroom, school nurse, run errands, and so forth. The routine stipulates whether the student can initiate use of the pass.

- A model of a completed assignment allows the autistic visual learner to better understand the expectations of the task. Models of assignments are also helpful for special educators and parents who may support the student to complete their work.

- Note-taking supports, which may include a complete outline that contains main ideas and details; an outline that contains main ideas with space (where the student fills in details); or a form that contains only outline numbers/letters (where the student adds main ideas and details).

- A Travel Card (Carpenter 2002) that lists four to five student behaviors that require ongoing monitoring across classes, such as (a) turned in homework, (b) brought supplies to class, (c) participated in class, (d) needed home base, or (d) followed schedule independently. The student carries this card from class to class, and each teacher indicates the student's performance during class, usually with a checkmark.

**Travel Card**
**Rocky**

Date ____________________

Key +=Yes 0=No NA=Not Applicable

| | Did student follow class rules? | Did student participate in class? | Did student complete assignments? | Did student turn in homework? | Teacher's initials |
|---|---|---|---|---|---|
| Reading | | | | | |
| Science | | | | | |
| Social Studies | | | | | |
| Study Skills | | | | | |
| English | | | | | |
| Spanish | | | | | |

| Bonus Points | Went to nurse after getting off bus? | | Has assignment book? | |
|---|---|---|---|---|

| **Total** | **+** | **0** |
|---|---|---|

*Teacher Comments/Suggestions/Announcements:*

*FIGURE 1.1*

- Check-in charts to enhance teacher awareness of their students' emotional states. As they enter each class, students complete a brief form that indicates how they feel.

*FIGURE 1.2: Gaffney (2024)*

Check-in charts may have negative effects for some. Because classroom teachers are not required to learn about and understand mental health challenges as a part of their university training (cf. Shelemy 2019), they feel ill-prepared to recognize and intervene in students' mental health challenges (cf. Panchal et al. 2022; Shelemy 2019). Further, a review of research on school-based mental health training programs showed little evidence that these programs improved teachers' skills to support students or increased student well-being (Anderson et al. 2018).

The aforementioned research offers a scenario of students who may do the following:

- Reflect on their mental health in classrooms with check-in charts.
- See their negative mental state magnified because of the amount of time they spend reflecting on it, thus increasing worry, stress, anxiety, and so forth.
- Expect teachers to provide support on these issues because that is what teachers do.
- Not receive intervention and support because teachers feel ill-qualified to do so.
- Feel helpless and hopeless because they are not supported by the teacher—who has signaled by the presence of the check-in chart that assistance will be provided.
- Have their mental state negatively affected because of their need for mental health support that is not forthcoming. This negative mental state may impact their (a) school attendance, (b) ability to learn, (c) math and reading scores, (d) interactions with peers and overall social adjustment, (e) grade point average, and (f) risk of substance abuse, sexual activity, and violence (Swick and Powers 2018).

Many autistic students experience negative emotions and/or mental health issues. In such instances, a personalized, as opposed to a class-wide, check-in chart may be helpful *if* the autistic has planned opportunities to meet with a *trained* mental health professional (e.g., social worker, counselor) who provides instruction on how to recognize feelings in self as well as identify and use supports.

Used without ongoing counseling and instruction, check-in charts may inadvertently increase student mental health challenges by directing students to dwell on their negative emotional states. As a result, these challenges may actually increase across time and spill over into other areas because classroom teachers are not trained to address students' needs.

## ***Classroom Visual Supports:***

Visuals supports are *necessary* for autistic students, but benefit *all* students. The benefits are many: increasing predictability, reducing behavior challenges, increasing attention to task, improving test scores, and increasing social interactions (Rutherford et al. 2020). The following presents a variety of visual supports that can benefit students throughout the day.

### **Visual Schedules**

Visual schedules offer a sequential presentation of upcoming activities in a concrete format and, as such, are compatible with autistic neurology (Rutherford et al. 2022). Specifically, they allow students to (a) anticipate upcoming events and activities even if they are nonreaders and (b) develop an understanding of time. In addition, they satisfy the need for predictability, reduce anxiety, and provide a greater sense of confidence about participating in an upcoming event (Rutherford et al. 2020; Vermeulen 2022). Further, visual schedules can be used to stimulate conversation through a discussion of past, present, and future events; increase on-task behavior; and facilitate transition between activities.

In classrooms that adhere to the use of evidence-based practices, a daily schedule is displayed that the entire class follows. The information listed in the schedule may be presented as follows:

- Solely through words
- Through words and pictures
- Entirely with pictures
- With objects that represent different locations and activities.

*FIGURE 1.3: Anonymous teacher (2024)*

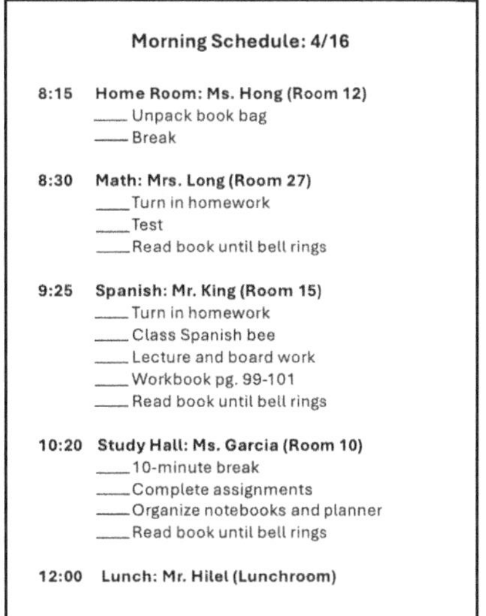

**Morning Schedule: 4/16**

**8:15 Home Room: Ms. Hong (Room 12)**
____ Unpack book bag
____ Break

**8:30 Math: Mrs. Long (Room 27)**
____ Turn in homework
____ Test
____ Read book until bell rings

**9:25 Spanish: Mr. King (Room 15)**
____ Turn in homework
____ Class Spanish bee
____ Lecture and board work
____ Workbook pg. 99-101
____ Read book until bell rings

**10:20 Study Hall: Ms. Garcia (Room 10)**
____ 10-minute break
____ Complete assignments
____ Organize notebooks and planner
____ Read book until bell rings

**12:00 Lunch: Mr. Hilel (Lunchroom)**

*FIGURE 1.4: Gaffney (2024)*

How do you determine which format to use? The schedule should be constructed in a way that allows students at various skill levels and with various learning styles to access the information.

More information on visual schedules may be found at https://ed-psych.utah.edu/school-psych/_resources/documents/grants/autism-training-grant/Visual-Schedules-Practical-Guide-for-Families.pdf.

## Posted Rules

Understanding and following rules is an essential skill for success in school, outside of school, and in adult life (Nuske et al. 2019; Øzerk et al. 2021). All students have fewer behavior challenges when the rules they are to follow are well constructed. Autistic students, because of their neurology, often have difficulty when rules do not communicate directly what the student should do. For example, a rule that says, "No blurting out," does not tell the student what to do to get the attention of the teacher. Additional information about writing, posting, and teaching rules may be found at https://autismclassroomresources.com/visual-rules-and-expectations-freebie/.

**Considerations When Developing Classroom Rules**

| Element | Description |
|---|---|
| **Specific** | State rules as concretely as possible. As much as possible, try to identify behaviors that can be observed. "Act appropriately," does not tell students what they are to do. |
| **Positive** | State rules in the positive rather than the negative. For example, instead of, "Don't yell in class," say, "Speak quietly in class." |
| **Publicly posted** | Design classroom rules that promote prosocial behavior by reminding students of classroom expectations. |
| **Few** | List no more than five rules. |
| **Matched to students** | Write rules at the students' reading comprehension level. Icons and pictures may be used in rules to increase understanding. |

*FIGURE 1.5: Adapted from Alter and Haydon (2017)*

| Considerations When Developing Classroom Rules *(continued)* | |
|---|---|
| **Element** | **Description** |
| **Input** | Solicit student input to increase student buy-in. Students also may identify issues that the teacher may not have considered. |
| **Taught and practiced** | Provide direct instruction on the rules, coaching, and multiple practice opportunities. |

*FIGURE 1.5 continued*

| Examples of Classroom Rules | |
|---|---|
| **Elementary** | **Secondary** |
| Be on time at the beginning of the day and after lunch or recess breaks. | Bring all supplies to class and have them ready to use (sharpened pencils). |
| Come prepared with supplies and completed homework. | Be at your desk and ready to do the first task when class begins. |
| Raise your hand to speak or to leave the classroom. | Begin any posted assignment at the very start of class. |
| Be kind, polite, and courteous to others. | Keep smartphones in your locker during school. |
| Keep your hands and feet to yourself. | Take care of out-of-classroom responsibilities before and after class. |
| Listen to the teacher and classmates, and follow directions. | Be polite in manner and speech; be kind to others. |
| Work hard, and always do your best. | Raise your hand to speak; do not blurt out. |

*FIGURE 1.6: Adapted from https://schools.magoosh.com/schools-blog/top-10-classroom-rules-for-elementary-school-students and https://classful.com/top-classroom-rules-for-high-school/.*

| Examples of Classroom Rules *(continued)* | |
|---|---|
| **Elementary** | **Secondary** |
| Be safe! | Behave in an honorable fashion; do not cheat. |
| Obey all school rules. | Begin to pack up five minutes before the day ends. You cannot leave though; the class lasts until the bell sounds. |

*FIGURE 1.6 continued*

## Routine Cards

One of the elements of a well-run and emotionally supportive classroom is the use of routines (Meindl et al. 2020). Agreeing, Kathy Quill (personal communication, August 4, 2005) notes that if educational professionals would spend the first two weeks of the school year teaching routines, students would have fewer challenges throughout the year. The concept of routines is compatible with autistic neurology: they are sequential, task-analyzed, visual, and consistent.

Routines should be created and taught for commonly occurring activities across the school day. Examples of routines to teach include how and when to (a) obtain forgotten supplies, (b) pass out papers, (c) hand in work, (d) sharpen your pencil, (e) get ready to go home, (f) clean out desk and backpack, and (g) transition from activity to activity.

A simple guideline: There should be a routine card for any regularly occurring direction that begins with "Get ready to" or "Clean out/up."

A good routine tells students the steps to complete a task. It also provides information about when to complete the routine. Good routines are as follows:

- Developmentally appropriate, culturally responsive, positively stated, specific, and observable.
- Explicitly taught, practiced, and reviewed.
- Presented in a visual format to enhance learning.
- Tied to positive reinforcement.

- Developed with students, when possible.

*Adapted from https://classroomcheckup.org/teaching-classroom-routines/ and https://www.teachstarter.com/us/blog/making-classroom-rules/.*

Leaving the Classroom

1. Line leader goes to door when the teacher calls their name.
2. Students lines up when teacher calls your row.
3. The teacher reviews the rules for walking to the new place: (a) stay with the group, (b) keep hands and body to self, and (c) use a whisper voice.
4. Teacher walks at the end of the line.

*FIGURE 1.7: Adapted from: http://idahotc.com/Portals/6/Docs/coaches%20institute/pbis_day4/3.AA%20Example%20Routines_elementary.pdf*

See Henry and Myles (2024) for more information about routines that require instruction and how to teach them.

## Voice Volume Scale

A *voice volume* scale is designed to help learners match voice loudness to the many environments they encounter throughout the day. The scale typically contains five volume levels each with (a) level number, (b) volume description, (c) picture of the level, and (d) where it is appropriate.

Not only does the scale allow students to understand voice volume across settings, but it also allows the support person to change students' voice volume nonverbally by pointing to the appropriate picture on the poster. In many schools, this voice volume scale is universally adopted so that students see it in the cafeteria, nurse's office, classroom, hallways, administrative offices, library, and other relevant settings.

Additional information about voice volume scales may be found at https://www.ocali.org/project/resource_gallery_of_interventions/page/Voice-Volume-Meter#:~:text=Voice%20volume%20meters%20can%20vary,a%20fun%20and%20engaging%20way.

| Voices in our Class | |
|---|---|
| 5 | **Yelling** - For outdoors...or in an emergency |
| 4 | **Loud Talking** – Usually too noisy |
| 3 | **Talking** – Regular talking |
| 2 | **Whispering** – Soft talking – also OK |
| 1 | **Silence** – No Talking at all |

*FIGURE 1.8: Gaffney (2024)*

**Problem-Solving Chart**

Recognizing that many autistics require direct instruction to use problem-solving skills (Herrero and Lorenzo 2020), Mataya and Owens (2012) created the Problem-Solving Rubric and Curriculum to teach learners to identify a problem and then use a specially designed chart to decide how to approach the situation.

Students are taught three typical solution options with multiple practice opportunities and coaching: (a) ignore it and move on, (b) let it bother you, or (c) seek help from an adult. An advanced option is introduced later: (d) talk it out and compromise. Finally, a scale with pictures is available for nonreaders who have not yet learned to compromise and a version for students who need to remove themselves to calm before participating in problem-solving. For more details and how to create and teach the problem-solving charts described above as well as others, see Mataya and Owens (2012).

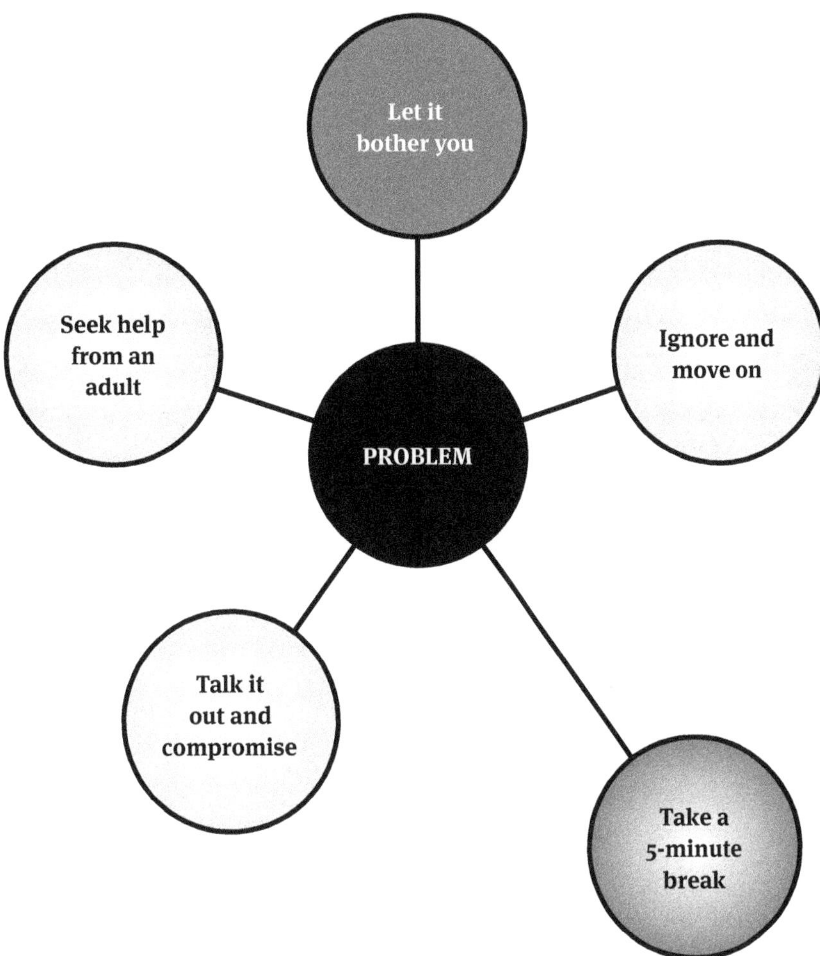


*FIGURE 1.9: Adapted from Mataya and Owens (2012).*

## Make Another Choice Card

The Make Another Choice Card is designed to help autistic students be successful. It provides a nonverbal redirection to a series of brief activities that will help the student focus. Tasks, which can be completed independently by the student, include the following: take a walk, do square breathing, get a drink of water, sharpen a pencil, scratch the Velcro inside your notebook, use a self-affirmation. The student chooses among the items listed on the Make Another Choice Card.

When teaching how to use this type of visual support, it is essential to make the student understand that this simple card helps to redirect them to an activity or break. It helps the student *not* get in trouble. This helpful two-sided card is subtly given to the student when they need redirection in the classroom, hallway, workplace, community, or home. See Henry and Myles (2024) for additional information.

FRONT BACK

*FIGURE 1.10: Gaffney (2024)*

**Boundary Markers**

Boundary markers are visual cues posted throughout the classroom that guide students through physical spaces (Uherek-Bradecka 2020). Visual boundaries are all around us across environments—cubicles in an office, cashier stations in grocery stores, booths in restaurants, lanes on a highway. Boundary markers not only help students understand their environment, but they often also provide a feeling of safety and comfort. With boundaries, learners know (a) where things begin and end and (b) what they can access without supervision (Mohamed and Alma 2024).

Boundaries can be created through furniture arrangement, labels, and color-coding. For example, a boundary for sitting could be a bean bag or pillow, or tape on the floor can show where to line up or where to place a chair. Other boundary markers include rugs, bookcases, other furniture, or colored tape on the floor that represent boundaries of areas for play and study.

Additional information on boundary markers may be found at https://www.simplyspecialed.com/visual-boundaries-in-your-autism-classroom/.

## *Social Supports*

This section of the Transition Checklist examines students' social environment as well as the instruction and supports that are needed to allow them to understand their surroundings and interact successfully with others.

## Bullying

About one quarter of general education students in high school experience bullying. Among bullied students, 15.5 percent miss one or more days of school because of safety concerns. This means that approximately six hundred thousand students are truant because of bullying (Steiner and Rasberry 2015). That is, more than half a million students do not feel safe in school. This is the start of a cycle.

These statistics point to what appears to be a connection between school absence and bullying:

- Students are more likely to report bullying if they did not attend school every day in the last two weeks.

- The proportion of pupils that were absent from school due to anxiety or mental health problems was higher among pupils that had been a victim of bullying.

- A longitudinal study found that the greater the incidence of bullying, the more likely the young person is to be truant. Young people who were bullied frequently were three times more likely to be truant than those who had not been bullied (Evans and Anti-Bullying Alliance 2023).

And the cycle continues.

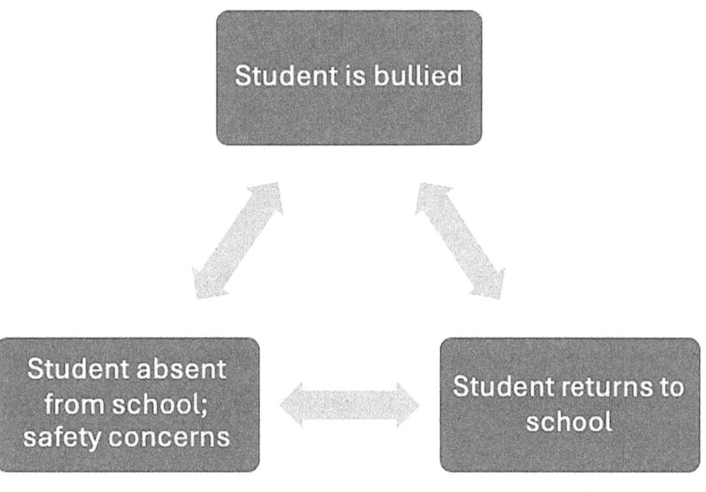


*FIGURE 1.11*

While bullying is clearly problematic for students in general education, it is an epidemic for students who require special education supports. Among these, the vast majority of autistic students are bullied (Hwang et al. 2018; Park et al. 2020), and its impact is both long-term and devastating.

Recent research has shown that bullied students show *chemical* changes in their brains which lead to long-lasting issues with the following:

- Fear
- Anxiety
- Physical illness
- Depression
- Decreased ability to self-regulate
- Lower academic performance
- Psychosis (Clemmensen et al. 2020; Okada et al. 2024).

## Hidden Curriculum

The *hidden curriculum* refers to the set of unstated rules that everyone knows, but that no one has been directly taught (cf. Myles et al. 2024). It includes (a) teacher expectations and assumptions, (b) multiple-meaning words, (c) idioms/metaphors, (d) nonliteral language, and (e) jokes/riddles. Also included in the hidden curriculum are almost all social skills because they are generally not directly taught and competence is automatically assumed.

Autistic students who are challenged to learn information that is not directly taught require direct instruction in the hidden curriculum to better understand their world. Some hidden curriculum items to teach include the following:

- How to use the urinal
- How to tell when the teacher "means business"
- That if you talk to teachers in a pleasant tone of voice they are more likely to respond positively
- How to tell when the teacher is happy with your performance
- That just because a person is popular does not mean they would be a good friend

Spending just two to three minutes per day to teach one hidden curriculum hidden item can have major results—students learning 180 unwritten rules at school and 365 items at home in a year's time. To that end, a special hidden curriculum calendar can make teaching and learning the hidden curriculum a very manageable task (Myles et al. 2025).

## Social Groups

When students are members of a group that provides successful social experiences, their mental health, academic skills, and social skills improve (cf. Fusar-Poli 2022). Thus, it is essential to identify key school-based social opportunities, such as Lunch Bunch, Circle of Friends, and special-interest clubs, that match student interests and strengths and provide support and instruction to ensure success.

| Potential Social Opportunities at School | |
|---|---|
| **Elementary** | **Secondary** |
| Lunch | Lunch |
| Recess | Hallways between classes |
| Playdates | Study halls/specials |
| Community-based clubs/teams | Extracurricular clubs teams |
| Family occasions | Community-based clubs/teams |

*FIGURE 1.12*

When creating social groups, the first consideration is how many students to include. The fewer people involved, the lower the social challenge. So, for students who are new to social groups, it may be best to start with a small number of peers and then expand as the student learns new skills.

When selecting neuromajority peers for a social group, consider those who have the following traits:

- Are of similar age
- Share similar interests
- Are motivated to participate in a social group
- Speak slowly
- Listen carefully
- Articulate clearly
- Express themselves directly
- Minimize the use of nonliteral language or explain it if they do
- Communicate their feelings
- Are entertaining and fun without mocking
- Are reinforcing
- Are dependable
- Genuinely like the autistic student
- Send a clear message of support (adapted from Loomis 2008).

After peers have been identified to participate in a social group, they must be trained. An understanding of autism, in general, and the student's autism, in particular, is helpful because once students understand each other, interactions are often easier. Neuromajority peers may also need to learn the following skills:

- How to gain the attention of the autistic student
- How to use language the autistic understands
- How to enhance motivation by offering choices

- How to model play and conversation skills
- How to encourage conversation and turn-taking
- How to reinforce the student
- How to use visual supports (Vanderbilt Kennedy Center 2022).

When the autistic student engages with peers in a social situation, it is important to provide ongoing supervision to ensure the group's goals are met and intervene as needed. In particular, the following should be observed and assessed.

| Considerations When Monitoring Social Groups | |
|---|---|
| **Elements** | **Observe** |
| **Proximity** | Does the student join the group? Remain near a peer? Stay by themselves? |
| **Enjoyment** | Is the student having fun? Is it just hard work? Or relaxing and enjoyable? |
| **Degree of interactions** | Is the student sitting beside or with peers? Sharing toys/objects? Participating in games/pretend play? |
| **Communication** | Is the student using verbal and nonverbal communication skills? Initiating and responding? Using voice volume and tone that matches the activity? |
| **Distress indicators** | Are there indications that social demands do not match the student's skills?<br>• Talking louder or faster than usual?<br>• Withdrawal?<br>• Acting uncomfortable?<br>• Other?<br><br>Are these behaviors precursors to a meltdown? |
| **Behaviors requiring instruction, support, coaching and/or multiple practice opportunities** | Is the learner engaging in behaviors that signal that additional instruction, support, coaching, and/or practice is needed in specific areas, such as follows:<br>• Manners?<br>• Listening?<br>• Hygiene? |

*FIGURE 1.13: Adapted from Loomis (2008); Vanderbilt Kennedy Center (2022).*

| Considerations When Monitoring Social Groups *(continued)* | |
|---|---|
| **Elements** | **Observe** |
| **Behaviors requiring instruction, support, coaching and/or multiple practice opportunities** *(continued)* | • Getting someone's attention?<br>• Topics to discuss beyond those of personal interest?<br>• Compromising? |
| **Predators** | Are there students who are likely to tease, bully, manipulate, or disrespect the learner? |

*FIGURE 1.13 continued*

## Social Skills Instruction

It is important to recall that the autistic brain is not wired to learn implicitly. As a result, autistic neurology requires direct instruction on skills that are typically not taught to the neuromajority. For example, the autistic student must be taught that the social skills needed by a third-grade student are different from those needed by a senior in high school. As a result, even if the third-grade student knows age-appropriate social skills to interact with their peers, it does not mean they will automatically have the skills to interact with students over the upcoming years.

Direct instruction using social skills curricula and social narratives allows students to better understand their environments and interactions with others. When creating activities, the following guidelines may help autistics enjoy and learn from social experiences:

- Target whatever motivates the learner
- Ensure that the student has the prerequisite skills to participate successfully
- Ensure that social demands are not too high and do not require too much effort
- Use humor, games, and fun activities
- Incorporate learner special interests, whenever possible
- Include people they like
- Be aware of signs of discomfort and be ready to support the student to achieve success.

## Social Skills Curricula

Several curricula designed for autistic students may be used to support student learning. Programs focusing on conversation skills are highlighted in the following because effective communication skills are the biggest predictor of successful independent living, having social relationships, and employment (Roux et al. 2015).

*Talk with Me: A Step-by-Step Conversation Framework for Teaching Conversation Balance and Fluency* (Mataya et al. 2017) was developed and refined across many years based on a review of the research along with close observation of how people talk to each other—what conversations really sound like. The Conversation Framework provides a simple, easy-to-implement process specific enough to equip an autistic individual with the tools necessary to acquire conversation skills and simple enough to be used at any age.

*Conversation Club: Teaching Children with Autism Spectrum Disorder and Other Social Cognitive Challenges to Engage in Successful Conversations with Peers* (Cannon et al. 2018) introduces conversation through a clubhouse filled with club members, including Friendly Freddy and Fix It Farrah. Students learn a variety of skills that facilitate thinking about the social significance underlying each conversation skill.

*Navigating the Social World: A Curriculum for Individuals With Asperger's Syndrome, High-Functioning Autism, and Related Disabilities* (McAfee 2013) contains a list of twenty social/emotional skills that address (a) recognizing and coping with one's emotions, (b) communication and social skills, (c) abstract thinking skills, and (d) behavior issues. This scope and sequence (and accompanying lessons) seems particularly appropriate for autistic girls. That is not surprising, as this resource was developed by a mother, a pediatrician, for her daughter.

## Social Narratives

Social narratives are simple stories that visually explain social situations and social behaviors. As such, they help the autistic student better understand the social context and their role in it. Social narratives are written to match individual abilities, attention span, and interests. They generally consist of the following elements (Henry and Myles 2024).

| Social Narrative | |
|---|---|
| **Elements** | **Observe** |
| Title | Who |
| Tailored to student's needs | What |
| Uses "I" or "he/she/they" | When |
| Uses past, present, or future tense | Where |
| Communicates a positive and patient tone | Why |
| Is literally accurate | How |
| May provide guidance on what to do | Others' perspectives |
| Often contains "I will try to" statements | Willingness |
| Uses words such as "usually," "sometimes," or "often" | Flexibility |

*FIGURE 1.14*

Social scripts, Social Stories™ (Gray 2016), the Power Card Strategy (Gagnon 2023), and social descriptions are all examples of social narratives. Additional information about developing and using the various social narratives may be found in Myles (2024) and at https://life-skills.middletownautism.com/background/teaching-life-skills/social-narratives/.

## Social Skills Interpretation

Even with the most thorough social skills instruction, autistic students inevitably encounter social situations they do not fully understand. As a result, they require someone who can interpret the encounter for them. These social skills interpreters act in a manner similar to that of language interpreters: They translate unfamiliar content into a form that is more easily understood by the observer or listener.

Several interpretation strategies help autistics understand their environment, including (a) cartooning, (b) social autopsies, (c) stop-observe-deliberate-act (SODA), and (d) sensory awareness.

## Cartooning

The term *cartooning* is often used to describe the use of drawings to help students learn social communication skills. Cartooning promotes social understanding by incorporating simple figures and other symbols in a comic strip format (People 2018; Reichow 2021), using color, conversation bubbles, and thought bubbles.

The Comic Strip Conversation (Gray 1994) is a type of cartooning. The author designed a conversation symbol dictionary that provides guidance on how to draw conversational elements, such as listening, interrupting, talking, using loud or quiet words, or thinking. Similarly, Arwood et al. (2015) offer guidelines for drawing cartoons, including:

- Using connected frames to illustrate sequence,
- Grounding the characters within the cartoon so there is no air between the person and the ground, and
- Making the drawn ideas move in one direction only.

Additional information about cartooning may be found at https://www.autism.org.uk/advice-and-guidance/topics/communication/communication-tools/social-stories-and-comic-strip-coversations.

## Social Autopsy

The *social autopsy* is an innovative strategy developed by Lavoie (Bieber 1994) to help students with social problems understand social mistakes. Simply stated, the social autopsy is a vehicle for analyzing a social skills problem. Following a social error, the student who committed the error works with an adult to (a) identify the error, (b) determine who was harmed by the error, (c) decide how to correct the error, and (d) develop a plan so the error does not occur again. This is a supportive and learning technique; it is not designed to punish students.

Every adult with whom the autistic student has regular contact, such as parents, bus drivers, teachers, custodians, and cafeteria workers, should know how to do a social skills autopsy fostering skill acquisition and generalization. Further information about conducting social autopsies may be found at https://www.youtube.com/watch?v=TyaHlOYtkI4.

## Stop-Observe-Deliberate-Act (SODA)

The social behavioral learning strategy SODA (Bock 2001 2007a 2007b) helps autistics "attend to relevant social cues, process these cues, ponder their relevance and meaning, and select an appropriate response during novel social interactions."

A visual strategy that has broad application, SODA utilizes the Think Aloud, Think Along model (Andrews and Mason 1991). It contains the following steps:

- **Stop.** This step prompts the student to develop an organizational schema in which an interaction is to occur. Specifically, the student attempts to define the activities and their order as well as identify a location near the activities from which they can observe to obtain additional information that will support successful participation in the activity.

- **Observe.** The student now observes the environment for clues to effective and successful interaction. Aspects targeted for observation may include length of conversations, number of individuals involved in conversations, tone of conversations (i.e., formal, casual), strategies to begin and end conversations, nonverbal language, and any routines that may be in place.

- **Deliberate.** In this phase, the student develops a plan to interact in the new environment. This includes deciding on a topic of conversation, identifying strategies that may lead to successful interactions (e.g., appropriately beginning a conversation, using eye contact, maintaining appropriate social distance), and analyzing how the student thinks they will be perceived by others if they do or do not follow the routines.

- **Act.** At this point, the student becomes an active participant in the novel environment, carrying out the strategies identified in the deliberation phase. This stage serves as a platform for generalizing skills that were learned in another environment.

SODA is not self-contained but relies on using social skills developed through direct instruction, coaching in group or individual settings, and multiple practice opportunities. It is one of the few strategies that supports students to approach unique situations without impulse and use social skills in a context that is appropriate. Additional information about SODA may be found at https://www.proquest.com/docview/205063437?pq-origsite=gscholarandfromopen view=trueandsourcetype=Scholarly%20Journals.

## Sensory Awareness

Many autistics experience the sensory aspects of their environment differently than their neuromajority peers. That is, because of their neurology, autistics may be over-sensitive or under-sensitive to specific sights, sounds, smells, or textures (cf. He et al. 2023). Depending on the circumstances, these sensory characteristics can be helpful but can also cause distress or discomfort, leading to meltdowns and an inability to function successfully.

Developing a sensory diet is one way to identify the specific needs of an individual (e.g., movement, touch, auditory) and subsequently provide appropriate sensory-based activities in a systematic, prescriptive manner (Pingale et al. 2019). With the assistance of an occupational therapist knowledgeable about sensory functioning, students can be taught how to understand their sensory systems and to incorporate sensory strategies into their daily activities to help them remain regulated (Myles et al. 2025).

Another approach is to help learners understand their sensory systems and the messages they convey. Mahler (2022) created *The Interoception Curriculum: A Step-by-Step Guide to Developing Mindful Self-Regulation* with this in mind. In this book, she introduces the eighth sensory system: interoception—the ability to notice and connect bodily sensations with emotions. Some autistics experience interoceptive signals that are so strong, they are immediately overwhelmed and confused. Others experience dulled or muted interoception signals that leave them unable to respond until they become immediate. This can lead to significant difficulties with emotional regulation and managing challenging behavior. The evidence-based (cf. Mahler et al. 2024), easy-to-use interoception curriculum systematically builds interoceptive awareness.

## *Academic Supports*

*Academic supports* provide the predictability and structure that make learning less stressful for autistic students. Helpful modifications discussed here include (a) priming, (b) assignment modifications, (c) note-taking, (d) graphic organizers, (e) enrichment, and (f) homework.

### Priming

*Priming* refers to preparing the student for an upcoming activity (Koegel et al. 2003). The learner who is primed is less likely to experience anxiety and distress about what lies ahead. With stress at a minimum, they can focus their efforts on successfully completing assignments and other activities (Meindl et al. 2020).

Priming involves a preview of activities and an overview of assignments or schedule changes—it is not a time to teach academic content. Priming begins with a review of the visual schedule so the day's structure is understood. The student may also be shown the actual materials that will be used in class, such as a worksheet or outline for a group project, so they can predict what will likely happen in each upcoming class (Canon et al. 2021).

Priming should occur close to when a given activity or lesson will occur. It may occur on the day before an activity, the morning of the activity, the class period before, or even at the beginning of the class period during which the activity will be completed. It can occur in school or at home. Anyone can prime the student—a teacher, a parent, or peer. Priming should occur in short, concise time periods in an environment that is relaxing for the student.

## Assignments

Similar to all other supports, assignment modifications should match the student's needs and may include the following.

- A student who works more slowly and methodically than peers may be allowed to complete fewer items.
- A student with handwriting issues may be allowed to complete assignments verbally or using a computer.
- A student who finds handwriting laborious may type an assignment or dictate it. A word bank or close-ended questions can be helpful for those who have difficulty retrieving information.
- A template or a sentence at the beginning of a writing assignment can help the student who has difficulty getting started.
- A model of a completed assignment can support a student who is challenged to translate the teacher's verbal instruction into something concrete.
- A highlighter can be used to draw attention to important information on worksheets or to indicate the items the student is to complete (Unknown n.d.).

Many ways other than traditional assignment and test formats exist to assess students' knowledge: collages, crossword puzzles, interviews, posters, brochures, video presentations, and so on. Additional information may be found at https://www.parentcenterhub.org/accommodations/.

## Note-Taking

Many autistic students have difficulty when required to take notes in class. Often, motor problems preclude them from getting important content onto paper in a timely manner. In addition, some students have difficulty listening and writing at the same time. Thus, note-taking alternatives are needed, and may include the following:

- A teacher-developed complete outline that includes main ideas and supporting details
- A teacher-developed skeletal outline that includes the main ideas and provides spaces for the student to fill in supporting details as these are discussed in class
- A peer-constructed outline developed by a fellow student
- Outlining software that allows the computer-adept student to take notes on main ideas and details.

If it is determined by the school team that it is in the student's best interest to take their own notes, instruction, coaching, and multiples must be provided. Additional information on this topic may be found at https://www.weareteachers.com/note-taking-strategies/.

## Graphic Organizers

Graphic organizers are tools used to provide visual representations of facts and concepts. As such, they arrange key terms to show their relationship to each other, presenting abstract information in a concrete manner. They are useful for explaining content-area material (e.g., social studies, science) or daily living skills (e.g., cooking, interviewing, dating).

These visual supports often enhance the learning of autistics because (a) they are visual—a frequent area of strength; (b) they are static; they remain consistent and constant; (c) they allow for processing time; the individual can reflect on the material at their own pace; and (d) they are concrete and are more easily understood than a verbal-only presentation.

Graphic organizers can be used to illustrate the following:

- **Columned charts** (also known as T-charts) can be used for examining pros and cons, similarities and differences, cause and effect, and what a character says compared to what they actually mean.

- **Concept maps** allow for exploration of a single concept. For example, a vocabulary word might be listed in the center, and the student might be asked to fill in the following information on the four surrounding squares: definition, the word in a complete sentence, synonyms, and a visual representation.

- **Venn diagrams** are primarily used to show differences and similarities in two or more concepts or items, for example, commonalities between mammals and amphibians.

- **Taxonomies** present the elements of a system, organization, or concept from the highest to lowest position. For example, they can be used to depict the main ideas and details of a story or the structure of the Continental Congress.

- **Cycle diagrams** show a series of events that have a beginning, middle, or end, such as the water cycle and life cycle of a butterfly.

- **Flow charts, timelines, and storyboards** perform a similar task: depicting a sequence of events or ideas. For example, timelines can show the beginning and end of the Tudor Era or the life of Jackie Robinson. Storyboards tell the beginning, middle, and end of a story.

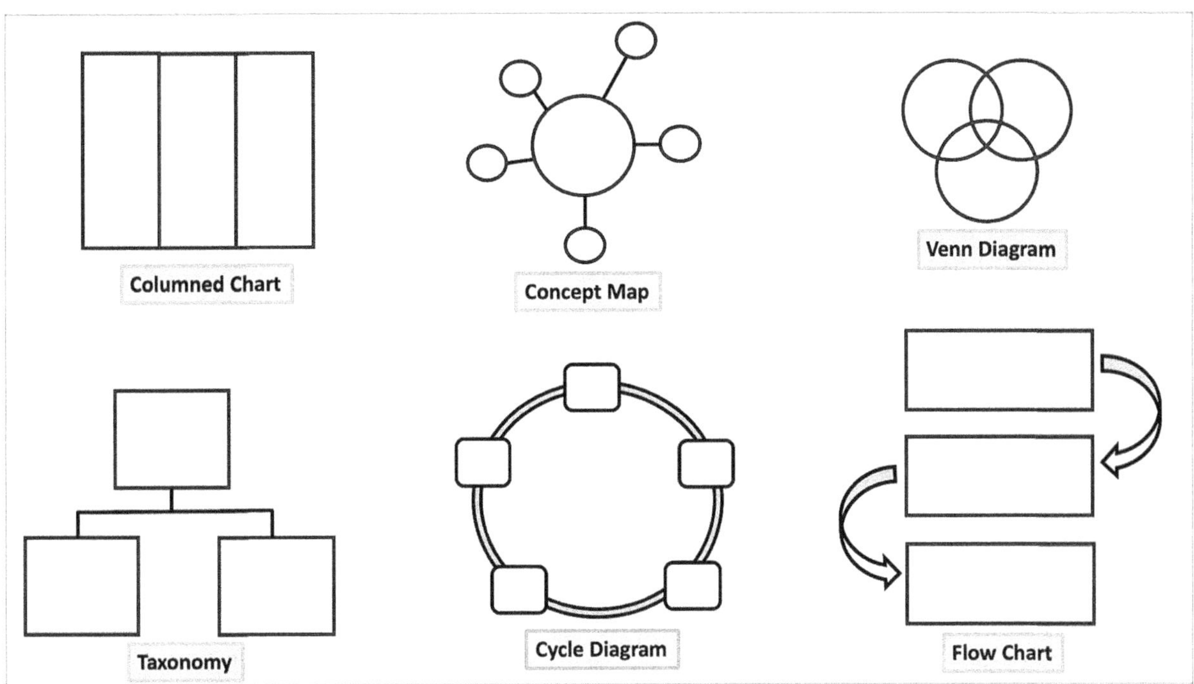


*FIGURE 1.15: Adapted from www.teachthought.com/critical-thinking/best-graphic-organizers/.*

To learn more about graphic organizers, please refer to https://www.theteachertoolkit.com/index.php/tool/graphic-organizers#:~:text=Graphic%20Organizers%20are%20useful%20educational,a%20visual%20display%20of%20information.

## Enrichment

One study found that around 60 percent of autistic individuals have special isolated skills and enhanced perceptual abilities (Meilleur et al. 2015). Similarly, research has shown that a greater percentage of autistic students have IQs in the superior or very superior range than found in the general population (Billeiter and Froiland 2023). However, too often the talents of autistic individuals are ignored amidst a focus on areas of need.

Enrichment is clearly needed, but how can we provide enrichment when the student has other skill areas that need to be addressed? Joli et al. (2020) suggest compacting to guide enrichment. *Compacting* refers to identifying student competencies, typically using pretests, and subsequently allocating time that would otherwise be devoted to those competencies to enriching activities. This can counteract the boredom and redundancy gifted students can feel when covering material they already know, replacing it with more meaningful work or independent projects (Matthews and Hujar 2021).

Enrichment supports include the following:

- Incorporating technology-aided instruction and intervention
- Mentorship and apprenticeship opportunities
- Researching areas of interest
- Incorporating extracurricular activities into the school day, such as chess or math club
- Learning contracts
- Community-based outings (cf. Nicpon et al. 2021)

Additional enrichment resources may be found at https://www.mada.org.qa/wp-content/uploads/2019/10/MADA_HFG-ENGLISH.pdf.

## Homework

Numerous challenges are inherent in assigning homework for autistic students (cf. Tamm et al. 2020). The most commonly reported homework problems include the following:

- The student did not write down the homework assignment.
- The student wrote down only part of the assignment.
- The student does not remember or know the details about the assignments that were given verbally in class.
- The materials necessary for completing the assignment did not come home with the student.

For these and many other reasons, it is often necessary to implement various adaptations to ensure successful completion of homework. The school team, including parents, may need to do the following:

- Identify key starting points for teaching the student to successfully complete homework.
- Depending on the needs of the student, develop a checklist of supplies and information needed for homework completion or teach the student a strategy to determine what supplies and information are needed.
- Using a visual support, teach the student the steps to organize homework for return to school.
- Create a visual routine for turning in homework.
- Prompt the student if the homework is not turned in.
- Reinforce the student.

## *Modifications for Unstructured or Less Structured Times*

For students who require structure to thrive, as is the case for many autistics, the unstructured or less structured times of the day pose the greatest problems. Riding the bus, physical education, lunch, changing classes, changes in routine, and before-/after-school times are difficult because they pose complex social demands with minimal structure. In addition, these times are often accompanied by a marked increase in sensory stimuli such as noise, touch, and smell that tend to cause dysregulation.

While problematic by themselves, all of these factors increase the chance that the autistic student will become dysregulated and, consequently, be teased or bullied. The latter is of particular concern because autistics are more likely to be teased, assaulted, or shunned than neuromajority children (Morton 2021; Park et al. 2020).

### Restrooms

There are many rules surrounding the use of public bathrooms—most of them untaught. Nevertheless, they are important, potentially impacting health and safety. Peter Gerhardt (personal communication, April 2004) talks about the rules associated with urinals. For example, if there is only one man at a urinal, a newcomer does not go to the urinal next to that person. Rather, he should go to a urinal that is at least two stalls away. Also, boys and young men should know that they are not to talk to someone while they are at the urinal and that they should never go to the bathroom in groups. Further, boys and young men should merely unzip to urinate rather than pulling down their pants at the urinal. Boys who pull down their pants could be open to victimization or be accused of exhibitionism.

This is just one of several complex bathroom rules. Violation of these rules can result in teasing, bullying, and other forms of victimization. Additional information about bathroom protocols may be found in Myles et al (2024).

### Transitions Within and Between Activities

*(Lee Stickle, MS, and Theresa Earles Vollrath, PhD)*

Transitions are a large part of any school day. Studies have shown that up a quarter of a school day may be spent engaged in transition activities, such as moving from classroom to classroom, coming in from the playground, going to the cafeteria, putting personal items in designated locations like lockers or cubbies, and gathering needed materials to start working (Bruck et al. 2022).

Transitioning between activities can pose difficulties for autistic students for several reasons:

- The steps of a transition are often assumed knowledge; educators often do not provide direct instruction, which is necessary for the autistic brain.
- Instructions, if provided, are often presented verbally—not the preferred mode for the autistic neurology.
- The subtle indicators of transitions are often not readily apparent to autistics, such as the teacher wrapping up a lecture or other students putting their away materials.
- Many transitions have a unique routine. Transitions from class to lunch, lunch to recess, and math to science each requires different steps.

Thus, transitions must be taught followed by coaching and multiple practice opportunities so they become automatic.

Assessing students' need for instruction in transitions requires that educators understand the nature of transitions (Bruck et al. 2022; Martinelli and Anderson 2024). There are three steps to each transition: (a) disengage, (b) shift, and (c) re-engage. To handle transitions successfully, students need to be fluent across all three stages.

1. In transition, to *disengage* means to stop at any given point in a task with little to no distress. Autistic neurology craves closure. Disengagement strategies help the autistic neurology by expanding the definition of closure.

2. To *shift*, or change or transfer to a new task, is often the most challenging part of the transition process. It is during the shift that most of us get "off track." There are different types of shifts. Some of these shifts can occur together or can occur independently.

3. The third part of the transition is to re-engage. Re-engagement is the *starting* point of the new task. This occurs when the learner begins to work on the new task (Stickle et al., n.d.).

| Transitions Within and Between Activities | | |
|---|---|---|
| **Step** | **Description** | **Elaboration and Examples** |
| **Disengage** | Stop the task | • When the entire task is finished.<br>• At a defined point in time even if all items, activities, or tasks are not complete; knowing that you may or may not go back to the task in the future. |

*FIGURE 1.16*

| Transitions Within and Between Activities *(continued)* | | |
|---|---|---|
| **Step** | **Description** | **Elaboration and Examples** |
| **Shift** | Change or transfer to the new task | • Within activity: Shifts that occur within the same task, such as shifting from hearing a lecture on math to completing an independent math assignment.<br>• New activity: Shifts that occur when transitioning between activities. For example, when a learner goes from math to reading.<br>• Nonmovement transition: Shifts that require the student to remain in one place, such as in the math activity described above. The student goes from listening to a lecture to doing an independent assignment while staying in the same location.<br>• Movement transition: Shifts that require the student to relocate, such as when going from listening to a lecture while sitting in their seat to a cooperative group assignment in math. |
| **Re-engage** | Start the new task | • When the student begins to work on the new task.<br>• Re-engagement is most successful when the lesson or activity is seen as "doable," interesting, and meaningful. |

*FIGURE 1.16 continued*

Students not only need to be taught the individual steps of each transition, but they also need to be able to disengage, shift, and re-engage for each transition. This likely requires multiple instruction and practice opportunities. See Henry and Myles (2024) for additional information on transitions within and between activities.

## Bus/Transportation

For autistic students, many aspects of getting to and from school by bus must be carefully analyzed to determine if modifications are necessary to ensure an uneventful, safe ride for everyone (Chan et al. 2022; Zepeda 2024), for example:

- What are the bus driver's rules and mannerisms? Often, bus rules are part of the hidden curriculum (see "Hidden Curriculum" in this chapter). This may mean that the student does not know how loudly they can talk and when talking is permitted.
- What is the noise level on the bus? On some buses, the noise level is high, which is often challenging for a sensitive sensory system.

- Do bullies ride the bus? The bus ride may provide opportunities for teasing and ridicule that are often not noticed by the bus driver, whose primary focus is on driving safely.

Not all autistics are challenged by the bus ride. But for those who are, decisions such as the following must be made by the school team and parents.

1. Is preferential seating needed (either near the bus driver or with a friend)?
2. Does the student know the bus driver's rules for conduct and talking?
3. Is the student aware of the consequences of breaking the bus driver's rules?
4. Does the student have the social skills necessary to talk with other kids while waiting for the bus and riding the bus?
5. Where does the student get assistance if they are being bullied or if they simply do not understand what to do?
6. Does the bus driver know about autism, in general, and the student's needs in particular?
7. Is an additional adult needed on the bus?

## Physical Education

While most neuromajority students enjoy physical education (PE) classes and sports programs as a diversion from sedentary academic classes, many autistics find this time of day stressful because of motor skill challenges and general difficulty with the concept of *team mentality*. The structure in PE may also be confusing to the autistic student (Kaplánová et al. 2022; Ruggeri et al. 2020). Often, the teaching staff operate under the assumption that all students know the rules for certain games, know where and how to line up, and understand how to win and lose graciously. They may also take for granted that everyone knows the language of PE.

The school team should consider whether, and under what conditions, a given student should participate in PE. Some students are successful in PE when the emphasis is on individual sports, such as cross-country running. Some students remain active in PE by serving as scorekeepers, equipment managers, and so on. If the student does participate in PE, the teaching staff must ensure that they understand the structure, rules, and language of PE and that they are included in all activities.

## Lunch

Like other unstructured or less structured times, lunch can be problematic for autistic students. As in PE, social and sensory demands as well as time constraints can make this portion of the day challenging and stressful. In fact, many autistics dread lunch, citing the smells and noise levels in the cafeteria and the other students as bothersome. Trying to juggle eating and talking within a twenty- to thirty-minute period can also be difficult. Added to these issues is the stress of trying to use newly acquired social skills to interact with others (Fujino and Ikeda 2023; Leifler et al. 2021).

The lunch period should be a comfortable time when students can eat, visit, and relax. If this is not the case, modifications may be needed. For example, if the student eats lunch in the designated lunchroom, they might need assigned seating with peer buddies near adult supervision and away from bothersome students and extreme noise. Also, peers could assist the student in navigating the lunchroom, going through lunch lines, getting silverware, paying, and so forth.

For some autistics, lunch is a successful experience if they are allowed to leave the cafeteria as soon as they are finished eating. However, despite such modifications, some adolescents become stressed and overwhelmed at having to eat in the cafeteria. For them, an alternative location, such as an empty classroom with peers, is a better option.

## Changing Classes

Passing time between classes causes great apprehension for many autistic students, given the limited time they have to get to their lockers, open them, decide what materials they need, gather these materials, and then make their way to the next class on time. The very nature of passing time is at odds with what many of us know about autism—"Twice the time, half as much done" (Myles et al. 2006). That is, autistics need more time than their neuromajority peers to accomplish tasks.

The school halls during passing time are chaotic. Often, there is not enough room to accommodate everyone milling around. Students brush up against each other to get where they are going, which can be misinterpreted and lead to frustration or an angry confrontation between students.

In addition to the specific recommendations regarding lockers below, a variety of modifications can make these transitions less frustrating:

- Early or late release from classes
- A peer who accompanies the student
- A five-minute warning from the teacher that the class is coming to an end to make changing classes more predictable

## Locker

Autistic students and their parents have identified the many misfits between school lockers and student needs and their impact on the student. They have emphasized that lockers are too small, locks are difficult to use, and lockers are placed in busy corridors that are noisy and overwhelming (Stack et al. 2020). The following strategies can be used to help students more easily access needed materials.

| Locker Usage | |
|---|---|
| **Locker Elements** | **Examples of How to Modify Locker Elements** |
| **Placement** | • Assign a locker at the end of the row so there won't be students on both sides of the autistic making access to the locker more difficult.<br>• Place the student's locker next to a peer who likes them.<br>• Assign lockers immediately outside or inside the class. |
| **Organization** | • Compartmentalize with shelves. Consider labels.<br>• Create a visual support that lists (a) class name, (b) teacher name, (c) room number, (d) books/supplies needed, and (e) when to visit locker. This visual support is inside each notebook.<br>• Color-code materials needed for each class: the math book has a red tab on the spine; the math notebook is red, a red pencil is Velcroed in the notebook.<br>• Place materials in the locker in the order they are needed. If the student takes books for two classes at once, encourage them to place them together in the locker. Consider placing a large rubber band around the two books. (Note: Have student carry extra rubber bands in the backpack.) |
| **Lock** | • Modify access to the locker for those who have difficulty with the standard lock due to fine-motor challenges. |
| **Locker Alternative** | • Consider a backpack on wheels to eliminate the need for a locker.<br>• Keep an extra copy of materials in each classroom. |

*FIGURE 1.17*

## Changes in Routine

Even when care is taken to ensure that routines are in place and that students know and understand them, sometimes routines are disrupted, which can be challenging for autistic students (Sheridan et al. 2023). To accommodate schedule changes, parents and the team must determine whether and how to prepare the autistic student for changes, including assemblies, fire drills, guest speakers, or seating changes. Students can be prepared for changes using a change card, a visual schedule, and/or social narratives.

One routine disruption—the substitute teacher—merits special attention. If the student experiences problems when there is a substitute teacher, arrangements may be made for them to remain with a familiar teacher, spend the day at home base, or complete work in the library or computer lab. See Henry and Myles (2024) for more suggestions on how to communicate schedule changes to students.

## Specials

Those who teach special subjects, such as art, music, and physical education, often report that they do not feel prepared to teach students who require social and academic supports to be successful (Begeske et al. 2023; Draper 2024).

Thus, these educators may need training and/or time to meet with the special educator to learn how to do the following:

- Create a predictable and visual routine that includes a visual schedule. This schedule is referred to when class begins and frequently throughout.
- Redirect the individual's attention when they are stuck.
- Know how to tell when the student needs a break.
- Structure activities that meet the student's needs. For example, if the student requires movement to stay focused, perhaps they can be asked to pass out and gather materials.
- Support the student to remain regulated using the strategies outlined in the student's program (see Chapter 2).

For additional information on using helpful supports in special subjects, please see Broupi et al. (2023) and Lamberti (2024).

## Before and After School

The time the student spends in school prior to the start of classes and the period between the last bell and when the student leaves school in the afternoon must also be considered to determine if modifications are needed. For example: Does the student need to be escorted to/

from the bus/car to class? Can the escort be a peer? And does the escort include stops at the nurse, locker, etc.?

At some schools, students arrive before they can access their classrooms. During this interval, the students congregate in the lunchroom, where there appears to be little structure. They can sit on the tables (!), sit on the benches, or stand around and talk to each other. They are permitted to play tabletop games (e.g., checkers, chess, paper football) that can be finished in a relatively short time. This structure often repeats during release time.

For students who may not thrive in this environment, several options are available:

- Students can be assigned to a different location (preferably with peers).
- Students can have preferential seating with a selected group of peers near adult supervision in the lunchroom.
- Students can be dropped off at school at the time when they can proceed directly to their lockers. Or they can be dropped off with early passing time to their lockers.
- Students can be provided a visual support of structured activities and their rules. In addition, a card of conversation starters might be helpful for promoting social exchange.

## Completion of the Transition Checklist

The Transition Checklist is completed by the student's sending team in the last few months of the school year. All of the student's sending teachers and parents should assist in filling out the checklist to ensure all relevant information has been included. Information from the learner's CAPS (if one exists; see the following chapter) and IEP can be used to complete the Transition Checklist.

## Summary

Creating a smooth transition for an autistic student requires thoughtful planning and preparation. The Transition Checklist capitalizes on the sending team's knowledge of the student by identifying the preparation, instruction, and supports that can help the student succeed in their new environment. Information from this easy-to-use tool is integral in the development of a plan that targets the student's strengths, needs, and interests.

# Chapter 1

## Transition Checklist: Creating a Successful Transition Experience—Revised

*Diane Adreon, EdD, and Brenda Smith Myles, PhD*

### PREPLANNING

*Conducting or Reviewing Assessments*

- ❑ Ensure that all staff who will be working with the student understand the student's strengths and concerns.

*Choosing Next Environment*

- ❑ Visit different types of programs, or programs at different schools, to determine appropriate placement options.

*Transition Planning Meeting*

- ❑ Create the student's schedule. Careful attention should be paid to choosing specials and creating opportunities for downtime where the student can engage in preferred activities to decrease anxiety levels.
- ❑ Create, review, and/or revise the IEP or 504 Plan to ensure that all necessary adaptations, accommodations, and modifications are included (e.g., homework, classwork, lunch, physical education, before school).
- ❑ Identify a teacher or administrator who will serve as the primary school contact for the parent to discuss any problems or changes that may occur.
- ❑ Schedule dates and content of training sessions for school personnel as needed. Plan to complete all training before school begins.
- ❑ Plan an orientation schedule for the student (see "Student Orientation").

*Training for School Personnel*

- ❑ Conduct a general orientation for all personnel at the school. This training session should include the following:
  - ❑ Overview of the characteristics of autism.
  - ❑ Information on the student's *specific* behavioral, academic, and emotional concerns.
  - ❑ All teachers, counselors, administrators, office staff, cafeteria workers, security, etc., who will have contact with the student.
- ❑ Provide training on how to implement the strategies determined during the transition planning meeting and/or included in the student's IEP. All teachers, counselors, and administrators in contact with the student should be present. This training session should include information on the following:
  - ❑ The specific step-by-step procedure to seek out the trusted person and get to home base.
  - ❑ The procedure to follow when a significant discrepancy exists between the individual's behavior and the environment using the Student Crisis Plan Sheet.
  - ❑ The procedure to ensure that homework assignments are recorded and that required materials are brought home.
  - ❑ How to implement all academic modifications, accommodations, and supports.
  - ❑ Other ________________________________________

From *Starting the School Year Well And What to Do If Things Go Awry* by Brenda Smith Myles, PhD & Diane Adreon, EdD (Future Horizons, Inc. - Arlington, TX - 2025)

*Student Orientation*

- ❑ Provide a walk-through of the student's daily schedule. For block schedules, the student should have the opportunity to practice all possible schedules. If applicable, student "buddies" should be available to walk through the schedule with the student. The following can comprise the walk-through:
    - ❑ Provide visual/written class schedule(s) for the student.
    - ❑ Videotape a practice school schedule for the student to review at home.
    - ❑ Practice route(s) from various classes/lunch to the bathroom, home base, etc.
    - ❑ Practice routines such as finding homeroom from the bus stop, opening the locker, going through the cafeteria line, etc.
    - ❑ Meet all teachers and relevant personnel.
    - ❑ Provide the student with pictures/names or video of all adults the student will have contact with (all educators, administration, cafeteria workers) in advance of the orientation.
    - ❑ Provide the student with pictures and names of student "buddies."
    - ❑ Show the student where the assigned seat in each classroom will be.
    - ❑ Obtain information about school routines and rules (e.g., lunch, rules about going to bathroom, before/after school, transportation).
    - ❑ Provide instruction on the procedure for seeking out the trusted support person and home base.
    - ❑ Practice use of transition to home base through role-play.

## ENVIRONMENTAL SUPPORTS

*Preferential Seating*

- ❑ Determine if preferential seating is necessary.
- ❑ Identify location.
- ❑ Identify supportive peers.

*Organizational Strategies*

- ❑ Determine the student's needs concerning organization of papers and materials.
- ❑ Provide assistance in organizing backpack, locker, and/or desk and teach the student to do so independently.
- ❑ Teach the student to use timelines.
- ❑ Instruct the student on how to develop a to-do list.
- ❑ Teach and support the student in cleaning out desk, locker, backpack.
    - ❑ Other ______________________________

*Home Base*

- ❑ Identify when home base will be used:
    - ❑ Before school or early morning
    - ❑ Following specific classes
    - ❑ On an as-needed basis
    - ❑ At the end of the day
    - ❑ Other ______________________________

- ❑ Determine cue to prompt home base.
- ❑ Determine home base location.
- ❑ Identify activities that will occur in home base.

*Trusted Support Person*

- ❑ Identify a trusted support person.
- ❑ Determine the role of the trusted support person, to possibly include the following:
    - ❑ Social skills instruction
    - ❑ Social skills interpretation
    - ❑ Active listening/empathizing
    - ❑ Calming the student
    - ❑ Sensory support
    - ❑ Other ______________________

*Personal Visual Supports*

- ❑ Identify which supports are needed:
    - ❑ Map of school outlining classes
    - ❑ List of classes, room #s, books, supplies
    - ❑ List of teacher expectations and routines by class
    - ❑ Classroom visual schedule (personal copy)
    - ❑ Mini-schedule for each class
    - ❑ Change symbol
    - ❑ Test reminders
    - ❑ Hall pass
    - ❑ Model of assignments
    - ❑ Outlines and notes from lectures
    - ❑ Travel card
    - ❑ Check-in chart

*Classroom Visual Supports*

- ❑ Visual schedule
- ❑ Posted rules
- ❑ Routine cards
- ❑ Voice volume scale
- ❑ Problem-solving scale
- ❑ Make another choice
- ❑ Boundary markers

## SOCIAL SUPPORTS

*Bullying*

- ❑ Who will monitor passing times, lunch, PE, restroom, and other areas where bullying is likely to occur.
- ❑ Identify anti-bullying program, if bullying is a problem.
- ❑ Identify peers to support the student at these times.
- ❑ Decide how bullying incidents will be addressed.
- ❑ Other ______________________________________________

*Hidden Curriculum*

- ❑ Identify hidden curriculum items.
- ❑ Identify who will teach the hidden curriculum.
- ❑ Determine when instruction will occur.

*Social Groups*

- ❑ Determine when Circle of Friends/Lunch Bunch/special interest clubs can be helpful.
- ❑ Identify peers to participate in social groups.
- ❑ Determine if peer training is needed.
- ❑ Identify who will create/expand social groups.
- ❑ Other ______________________________

*Social Skills Instruction*

- ❑ Determine need for direct instruction.
  - ❑ Identify curricula.
  - ❑ Determine social skills instructor.
  - ❑ Determine when social skills instruction will occur.
  - ❑ Identify coaches/teachers who require training.
  - ❑ Provide awareness training to other students.
- ❑ Consider whether social narratives (social scripts, Social Stories, Power Card Strategy, social descriptions) enhance instruction.
  - ❑ Identify individual who will create social narratives.
  - ❑ Determine who will train others to use the social narrative.
  - ❑ Determine who will monitor social narrative effectiveness.

*Social Skills Interpretation*

- ❑ Identify social skills interpreter.
- ❑ Ensure social skills interpreter knows how to use (a) cartooning, (b) social autopsies, (c) SODA, and (d) sensory awareness.
- ❑ Identify when student will have access to the social skills interpreter.

## ACADEMIC MODIFICATIONS

*Priming*

- ❑ Determine whether priming will help meet the student's need for predictability.
- ❑ Analyze student needs and classroom demands to determine which classes will require priming.
- ❑ Identify who will conduct the priming.
- ❑ Designate whether priming will use actual or similar materials.

*Assignments*

- ❑ Determine the student's needs concerning assignments.
  - ❑ Provide the student with extra time to complete assignments.
  - ❑ Shorten the length of assignments.
  - ❑ Read directions to/with student.
  - ❑ Reduce the number of assignments.
  - ❑ Break assignments into smaller segments.

- ❑ Provide models of completed assignments and/or a list of specific criteria for successful completion.
- ❑ Allow the student to use the computer for schoolwork and/or homework.
- ❑ Allow the student to demonstrate mastery of concepts through alternate means (dictate essays, oral tests, etc.).
- ❑ Provide alternatives to handwriting; specify ____________________
- ❑ Other ____________________

*Note-Taking*

❑ Indicate the type of note-taking supports needed by the student.

- ❑ Provide a complete outline.
- ❑ Give student a skeletal outline.
- ❑ Identify a peer who can take notes for the student.
- ❑ Allow the student to use outlining software.
- ❑ Other ____________________

*Graphic Organizers*

❑ Determine if graphic organizers are needed to facilitate skill acquisition and maintenance.

*Specify which type of graphic organizers will be needed:*

- ❑ Columned chart
- ❑ Concept map
- ❑ Venn diagram
- ❑ Cycle diagram
- ❑ Other ____________________

*Enrichment*

❑ Determine the type of enrichment needed.

❑ Determine when and how enrichment will be provided.

❑ Decide whether a learning contract with specified working conditions is needed.

❑ Other ____________________

*Homework*

❑ Identify which class subjects will include homework responsibilities.

❑ Determine homework modifications.

- ❑ Present homework assignments visually (on board, etc.) in addition to orally.
- ❑ Provide the student with a homework sheet or planner.
- ❑ Provide peer or teacher assistance in recording homework assignments.
- ❑ Reduce the amount of homework.
- ❑ Provide a study hall period to complete homework at school.
- ❑ Other ____________________

- ❑ Identify home strategy for completing homework.
  - ❑ Designate place and time for homework completion.
  - ❑ Define how student will get homework back to school.
  - ❑ Identify contact if additional clarification is needed on homework.
  - ❑ Other ______________________________

## MODIFICATIONS FOR UNSTRUCTURED OR LESS STRUCTURED TIMES

*Restrooms*

- ❑ Ensure that student knows bathroom rules (e.g., which urinal to choose, whether to talk, protocol for using the bathroom).

*Transitions Within and Between Classes*

- ❑ Within Classroom Transitions (i.e., from reading to math in the same classroom):
  - ❑ Identify who will create a classroom transition routine.
  - ❑ Identify who will teach the transition routine.
- ❑ Between Class Transitions (i.e., moving to another classroom):
  - ❑ Determine who will provide a list of transition steps for each class.
  - ❑ Determine if a peer to accompany during transitions is helpful.
- ❑ Identify who will teach the transitions.

*Bus/Transportation*

- ❑ Identify who will teach the bus routine.
- ❑ Determine who will support the student when the bus arrives at school, particularly on the first day of school. For at least the first week, have a peer or staff greet the student at the bus and accompany them to the bus at the end of the day.
- ❑ Determine how long assistance will be needed in getting to and from the bus.
- ❑ Identify peers or school personnel who will assist the student in this process.
- ❑ Provide a pickup or drop-off closer to the student's house.
- ❑ Provide adult supervision at the bus stop.
- ❑ Provide a peer "buddy" from the student's neighborhood to wait with the student at the bus stop and sit with the student on the bus.
- ❑ Provide preferential seating on the bus. This may include seating the student near the driver or allowing her to sit in her own seat/row.
- ❑ Provide a monitor/aide on the bus.
- ❑ Provide individualized transport (please describe). ______________________________
- ❑ Other ______________________________

Physical Education

- ❑ Consider whether to exempt the student from PE and, if so, substitute another special or a study hall. This is important if poor motor skills have led to teasing or rejection by peers.

- ❑ Assign the student a specific role for PE such as scorekeeper, equipment manager, etc.
- ❑ Assign teams rather than allow students to choose teams themselves.
- ❑ Have school personnel monitor, at least twice weekly, the student's perceptions of the PE period by asking them how they feel the period is going.
- ❑ Help the student problem-solve difficulties.
- ❑ Other ______________________________

*Lunch*

- ❑ Have school personnel available during the first week of school to assist the student in navigating the cafeteria line, finding a place to sit, and engaging in an appropriate activity once they are finished eating.
- ❑ Help the student identify school personnel they can approach during the lunch period when encountering problems.
- ❑ Have school personnel closely monitor student's (a) interactions with peers and (b) stress levels, and intervene when problems occur.
- ❑ Have school personnel monitor, at least twice weekly, the student's perceptions of the lunch period by asking the student how they feel the period is going.
- ❑ Provide assigned seating with a preferred peer, away from problem peers and/or near adult supervision.
- ❑ Provide a peer "buddy/buddies" during lunchtime.
- ❑ Allow the student to leave the cafeteria after eating, to engage in a calming or preferred activity (e.g., go to media center, computer lab).
- ❑ Allow the student to eat lunch in an alternative location.
- ❑ Other ______________________________

*Changing Classes*

- ❑ Provide peer or teacher help (particularly during the first week) to help the student manage crowded hallways, open locker, locate the proper materials, and find the correct classroom.
- ❑ Provide a peer "buddy" to accompany the student during class changes if they continue to have trouble during this time. This "buddy" might assist the student with organizational issues, protect against bullying by other students, and promote positive social interactions.
- ❑ Provide the student with additional time for class changes.
- ❑ Allow alternate passing time when the hallways are free from other students. For example, the student might change classes before or after the general transition period.

*Locker*

- ❑ Identify student's locker needs:
  - ❑ Consider backpack on wheels.
  - ❑ Traditional locker.
  - ❑ Add shelves/dividers.
  - ❑ Consider lock modifications (i.e., laser opener, extra key).
  - ❑ Practice using locker.
  - ❑ Placement: _____ Near a friend _____ End of row
- ❑ Identify who will teach and monitor.
- ❑ Other ______________________________

*Changes in Routine*

- ❑ Specify whether the student needs to be informed of any changes in typical classroom procedures (assemblies, fire drills, guest speakers, seating changes, substitute teacher).
- ❑ Determine what additional supports the student needs when changes occur.
- ❑ Other ______________________________

*Specials*

- ❑ Consider acting lessons/drama class.
- ❑ Create structure in specials classes similar to those in academic classes (i.e., visual schedule, routines).
- ❑ Identify who will train specials teachers, if needed.
- ❑ Provide structured activities.
- ❑ Other ______________________________

*Before and After School*

- ❑ Identify when the student should arrive at school.
- ❑ Determine whether a specific room should be used during this time.
- ❑ Identify peers to support the student at this time.
- ❑ Provide structured activities.
- ❑ Other ______________________________

From *Starting the School Year Well And What to Do If Things Go Awry* by Brenda Smith Myles, PhD & Diane Adreon, EdD (Future Horizons, Inc. - Arlington, TX - 2025)

# Chapter 2

# Comprehensive Autism Planning System

The Comprehensive Autism Planning System (CAPS) provides an overview of a student's daily schedule by time and activity as well as the supports the student needs during each period. CAPS is often referred to as the "practical" IEP—it simply details what supports the student needs, when they are needed, and what they look like. For example, the CAPS allows the math teacher, at a glance, to identify how to create a successful learning environment for the autistic student.

## Description

The CAPS is designed so that the supports and interventions can be easily implemented across each environment. Thus, the CAPS allows professionals and parents to answer the all-important question for autistic students: What supports does the student need for each activity?

Following the development of the student's IEP, all educational professionals who work with the student create the CAPS. Each teacher then keeps the student's CAPS at ready access—on their electronic device (e.g., computer), on their desk, or in a notebook.

The CAPS consists of a list of a student's daily tasks and activities, the times they occur, and a thorough delineation of the supports needed to support success. In addition, it includes space for making notations about data collection and how skills are to be generalized to other settings.

### *Time*

This section indicates the clock time when each activity that the student engages in throughout the day takes place.

### *Activity*

This includes activities throughout the day in which the student requires support. Academic periods (e.g., reading, math), nonacademic times (e.g., recess, lunch), and transitions between classes are all considered activities.

### *Skills to Teach*

This area may include IEP goals, the Common Core, and/or general skills that lead to school success. Skills may also be identified by parents or the student. These skills can serve as the basis for measuring response to intervention (RTI) or annual yearly progress (AYP).

### *Structure/Modifications*

Structure/modifications encompass a wide variety of supports that may include restructuring the environment, changing academic requirements, and teaching new skills.

| Examples of Structure/Modifications That Might Appear on the CAPS | |
|---|---|
| Daily schedule | Fewer problems to solve |
| Mini-schedule | Use keyboard instead of writing by hand |
| Choice board | Take tasks in a quieter location |
| Work system | Audiobook with textbook |
| Priming | Self-monitoring |
| Carpet square | Circle items to complete |
| Early/late release with peer | Locker shelves |
| Voice volume scale | PE dress out in private |
| Problem-solving scale | Tests read to student |
| Oral response | Multiple-choice instead of essay questions |

*FIGURE 2.1*

### *Reinforcement*

Student access to specific types of reinforcement as well as reinforcement schedules is listed under this section. While other sections of the CAPS may be left blank because the student does not need additional support, the reinforcement section should *never* be left blank. All students need reinforcement. Reinforcement helps ensure that the skill demonstrated by the student occurs again.

| Examples of Reinforcers That Might Appear on the CAPS | |
|---|---|
| **Types** | **Examples** |
| Special interest items | Books, podcasts, computer research |
| Sensory items | Wind-up toys, music, crunchy foods, inflatable cushion |
| Social/leisure items | Take a break, time with a preferred peer, skip one assignment, play a game with a peer |
| Tangible/edible items | Certificate, cool school supply, hobby trading card, healthy snack |

*FIGURE 2.2*

### *Sensory/Regulation*

Supports that help the student remain focused, calm, and comfortable in their environment are placed on the CAPS under the Sensory/Regulation category. They are often identified by an occupational therapist, special educator, Board Certified Behavior Analyst (BCBA), and others who understand the sensory systems and the many facets of regulation.

| Examples of Sensory/Regulation Supports That Might Appear on the CAPS | |
|---|---|
| Earbuds/noise-canceling headphones | Stress thermometer/emotion level chart |
| Movement breaks | Self-management routine card |
| Fidgets | Home base and hall pass |
| Exercise bands | Calming social narrative |
| Chewy tube/gum | Antiseptic bouncing |

*FIGURE 2.3*

| Examples of Sensory/Regulation Supports That Might Appear on the CAPS *(continued)* | |
|---|---|
| Music | Just walk and don't talk |
| Ball chair | Body check chart |
| Inflatable seat cushion | Visual self-calming routine |
| Slant board | Make another choice card |

*FIGURE 2.3 continued*

### *Communication/Social Skills*

Specific communication goals or activities as well as corresponding supports are delineated here. Goals or activities may include (a) requesting help, (b) taking turns in conversation, or (c) protesting appropriately. Social goals may include learning to share space, share focus, and share enjoyment (Taylor et al. 2024).

<table>
<tr><th colspan="2">Examples of Communication/Social Skills Supports That Might Appear on the CAPS</th></tr>
<tr><td colspan="2">Augmentative and alternative communication (AAC) systems<br>• Sign language<br>• Low-tech systems, such as the picture exchange communication system (PECS; cf. Bondy and Frost 2001: Danker et al. 2023) and interactive communication boards<br>• High-tech systems, including voice output communication aids (VOCA)/speech generating devices (SGD)</td></tr>
<tr><td>Social routines visual</td><td>Cooperative groups</td></tr>
<tr><td>Video models of social/communication skills</td><td>Circle of Friends/Lunch Bunch/peer buddies</td></tr>
<tr><td>Social narratives</td><td>Emotions words dictionary</td></tr>
<tr><td>Conversation skills visual support</td><td>Cartooning</td></tr>
<tr><td>Conversation starter card</td><td>Social autopsy</td></tr>
<tr><td>Emotions words visual</td><td>Hidden curriculum—one item per day</td></tr>
</table>

*FIGURE 2.4*

## *Data Collection*

This includes gathering information on behavior(s) to be documented during a specific activity. Typically, this section relates directly to the student's IEP goals and objectives, behavioral issues, and state standards. The more specific the data collection, the more likely data are to be collected and be useful to track student progress.

| Data Collection Parameters | | |
|---|---|---|
| **Information Needed** | **Variables to Consider** | **Examples** |
| **Days to Collect Data** | M, T, W, Th, F | M/15m/#/Requests<br>On Mondays, collect data for 15 minutes on student requests using event recording |
| **Time Length** | 15m, 1h | TandW/10m/In seat<br>On Tuesdays and Wednesdays, collect data for 10 minutes on time in seat using duration recording |
| **Data to Collect** | # event recording duration recording 🕒 | |

*FIGURE 2.5*

### *Generalization to Community*

Because autistic individuals tend to narrowly apply information they have learned, emphasis must be placed on helping them generalize. This section of the CAPS was developed to ensure that generalization of skills and supports is built into the student's program. Examples are detailed in the following (LaCava 2024).

| Generalization of Supports | | | |
|---|---|---|---|
| **CAPS Categories** | **Support** | **Is Used During ...** | **Can Also Be Used During ...** |
| **Structure/ Modifications** | • Circle problems to be completed on a worksheet<br>• Audiobook | • Math<br>• Reading | • Science, read-ing, social studies, PE, music<br>• Social studies, science |
| **Sensory/Regulation** | • Slant board<br>• Therapy ball | • Language arts<br>• PE | • Math class, art<br>• Reading, math, social studies |
| **Social/ Communication** | • Social script<br>• Language board | • Attendance<br>• Specials | • Academic times: ask a peer to work on a project, initiate interactions with cooperative group members<br>• Any other setting |

*FIGURE 2.6*

| Generalization of Skills | | |
|---|---|---|
| **Skill to Teach** | **Is Used During ...** | **Can Also Be Used During . .** |
| **Asking for help** | General education academic time | Recess, lunch, when completing daily living skills |
| **Using a calculator** | Math, science | Grocery store, bank, school store, on a computer or smart device |
| **Interpreting facial expressions** | Social skills group | Recess, lunch |

*FIGURE 2.7*

A copy of the CAPS appears at the end of this chapter.

### *The Modified Comprehensive Autism Planning System (M-CAPS)*

The CAPS can also be used in middle and high school with some modifications due to structural differences across the school years. While elementary-age students often remain in the same setting all day or infrequently move from class to class except for some specials, for example, most secondary students change rooms and teachers for each class. They may have as many as nine teachers in nine different classrooms during a typical school day. Despite their movement from classroom to classroom, the activities in which students participate in each academic class are similar.

In each class, secondary students are likely to be required to participate in a mixture of independent work, group work, tests, lectures, and homework. So instead of listing each academic and nonacademic task under the Activity section as is done on the CAPS, the Modified-Comprehensive Autism Planning System (M-CAPS) lists the following:

- Independent Work
- Group Work
- Tests
- Lectures
- Homework
- Transitions, if supports and instruction are needed (This instrument appears at the end of the chapter.)

From this standpoint, the activities in English class and geometry are typically the same. But on occasion, there may be minor differences in needed supports. For example, a student may need a calculator for all mathematics-related classes but not for those that are primarily reading based. All other supports are most likely identical across classes. This has many benefits:

- The supports can be made en masse by a paraprofessional under the direction of a special educator. All educators can be supplied with one or more than one copy (in case of loss or wear) of each support.
- All educators can learn about the supports and practice using them in a professional development session.
- Because they share identical supports, academic teachers are more likely to collaborate about their shared student(s) and the impact of the supports.

But despite the above differences, some classes in middle and high school mirror in structure those that are taught in elementary school. For these classes, the traditional CAPS may be used.

Physical education, lunch, and bus are examples of classes for which the traditional CAPS by time and activity would be most appropriate. Students who have work experiences, community-based opportunities, and extracurricular activities would also have a traditional CAPS completed for these classes.

Thus, some secondary students may have an M-CAPS for their academic classes and a CAPS for nonacademic activities.

### *Benefits of CAPS and M-CAPS*

CAPS and M-CAPS have many benefits:

- These clearly developed plans with pictures of supports can help the receiving team develop a plan for the upcoming year.
- They help ensure that students' needs are met across the school day.
- They were founded on the recognition that autistic students have complex strengths and needs in multiple areas, including structure/modifications, reinforcement, sensory/regulation, and communication/social skills. All must be addressed in order for the student to reach their limitless potential
- They are built on a collaborative model. Collaboration ensures that all adults understand the student and know how to best support their learning. Collaboration also reduces redundancy. This is important because it seems that there are never enough resources—and likely never will be.
- They include assessments designed to increase student achievement. That is, a data collection component accompanies each skill that the student is taught. Such skills may include IEP goals as well as the state standards. As a result, data are collected throughout the student's day across all settings.

- They recognize that social/emotional/behavioral issues impact every aspect of the student's day. In fact, the CAPS and M-CAPS require that the IEP team, including parents, identify social/emotional/behavioral and communication supports for each class, each transition between classes, and before and after school.
- They support meaningful instruction and generalization by identifying the goals and supports the student needs for each activity.
- They embed evidence-based instructional strategies within the student's daily schedule to ensure progress throughout the day.
- They can support autistics throughout life. That is, while CAPS and the M-CAPS can be used at the elementary and secondary levels, respectively, they can also be used for postsecondary education, employment, activities in the community, and home.

## Completion of the CAPS and M-CAPS

The CAP and M-CAPS, that show instruction and supports necessary for student success, are completed by school team members annually with updates as needed throughout the year. These forms support student transitions by providing a detailed plan of the student's program. The sending team shares the CAPS and/or M-CAPS with the receiving team, who in turn uses this information (and other resources identified in this book) to develop a new CAPS and/or M-CAPS that creates a match between the student's strengths/needs/preferences and the environment.

## Summary

The CAPS and M-CAPS ensure that students have the supports and instruction to be successful without the expenditure of a great deal of time to develop and implement. In addition, the success created by using CAPS and M-CAPS is sustainable. That is, the two tools can be used beyond the school environment—to support success in postsecondary education, on the job, in the community, and at home. Further information about CAPS and M-CAPS may be found in *CAPS: Comprehensive Autism Planning System* (Henry and Myles 2024).

# Comprehensive Autism Planning System (CAPS)

Student's name: ______________________ Date: ______________
SS = state standards

| Time | Activity | Skills to Teach | Structure/ Modifications | Reinforcement | Sensory/ Regulation | Communication/ Social Skills | Data Collection | Generalization to Community |
|---|---|---|---|---|---|---|---|---|
| | | | | | | | | |
| | | | | | | | | |
| | | | | | | | | |
| | | | | | | | | |
| | | | | | | | | |
| | | | | | | | | |

From *CAPS: Comprehensive Autism Planning System* by Shawn Henry & Brenda Smith Myles, PhD (Future Horizons, Inc. - Arlington, TX - 2024)

# Modified Comprehensive Autism Planning System (M-CAPS)

Student's name: ______________________ Date: ______________
SS = state standards

| Activity | Skills to Teach | Structure/ Modifications | Reinforcement | Sensory/ Regulation | Communication/ Social Skills | Data Collection | Generalization to Community |
|---|---|---|---|---|---|---|---|
| **Independent Work** | | | | | | | |
| **Group Work** | | | | | | | |
| **Tests** | | | | | | | |
| **Lectures** | | | | | | | |
| **Homework** | | | | | | | |

# Chapter 3

## Learner Snapshot

Information provided by parents about their child is essential when planning a student's school program. Because they have known their child longer than any educator and have observed their child in multiple environments under various conditions, parents' descriptions are valuable, potentially saving educators hours in program planning and getting to know the student. The special education coordinator asks parents to complete the Learner Snapshot at the end of the year, and the form is distributed to staff during the initial training prior to the first day of school so staff unfamiliar with the student can read it prior to the student beginning the new grade or school.

### Description

The Learner Snapshot provides a structured way for parents to share information about their child that may be helpful in planning the student's program, structuring motivating activities, and facilitating a positive relationship between the student and teacher. A brief description of each section of the form follows. A copy of the Learner Snapshot is included at the end of the chapter.

#### *Exceptionality Description*

Every student is unique, and using one word to describe them is often not helpful in developing a successful school program. This is especially true for students with autism, because autism looks different in each person. Labeling someone as autistic does not adequately describe them.

The following questions may help parents come up with an answer to this section:

- What does your child's autism look like?
- Does your child have any co-occurring issues, such as anxiety, depression, attention issues, or intellectual disability?

- Does your child receive any therapies outside of school?
- Does your child take any medications that may impact them at school?

### *Family Description*

Family descriptions are also important to educators. They provide information that can be used to (a) develop a relationship with the student, (b) motivate or reinforce the student, (c) make lessons and activities motivating and familiar, and (d) develop a partnership with parents to benefit their child's education.

Questions that can be used to guide the interview include the following:

- Who is in your family home?
- What are sibling names and ages, as appropriate?
- Are there extended family members that the student is especially fond of?
- Do you have pets?
- Does the family or child participate in indoor or outside activities that you would like to share?
- Are there any family issues that you would like to discuss that might impact your child in school, such as (a) a parent may travel frequently, which upsets the child, (b) the child may become distracted for a day or two when grandparents return home after visiting, (c) a family member is divorcing, or (d) the family has recently moved.

### *Learns Best*

Not only is it important to know the student's skill levels in various areas, but it is also essential to identify how they learn. With this information, educators can structure activities in ways that streamline the student's learning.

The following questions can support parents in sharing information about their child's learning:

- How does your child learn? Do they best learn and remember information when they (a) see it in words, (b) see it in pictures, (c) hear it, (d) do it with you, (e) have something they can hold on to, or (f) other?
- Do you find it helpful to prepare your child when something is about to happen, such as going to the grocery store or getting ready for bed? If yes, please describe how you prepare your child.
- What information does your child seem to learn quickly?

- What types of skills does it take longer or more practice for your child to learn?
- Do you use pictures, lists, checklists, schedules, or other supports with your child? If yes, please describe them.

### *Special Interests/Preferences/ Motivators*

Most people have some sort of hobby, interest, or area of expertise. So do autistic people. Topics regarded highly by autistic people, often referred to as *special interests*, can be very intense and sometimes all-consuming. They can include common topics, such as television shows and trading cards, or unique subjects, such as albino bats and vacuum cleaners. Using special interests in school activities positively impacts the learning, attention, social interactions, and self-esteem of autistics.

Special interests, preferences, and motivators can be identified using the following questions as a guideline:

- Does your child have any strong or special interests? What are your child's interests and preferences?
- What do they enjoy during their free time?
- What does your child like to do with peers?
- What sort of things reinforce or reward your child: computer time, book or magazine time, drawing/coloring, time with a peer, helping the teacher, music, sensory items, movement, high fives, games or puzzles, blowing bubbles, shredding paper, taking a walk, food?
- What is likely to help your child pay attention or stay on task: short tasks, frequent breaks, listening activities, activities that include a special interest, activities that do not include writing, group activities, activities where the student can move or be active, activities on a certain subject, having a schedule, being prepared in advance, other?

### *Strengths*

Learner strengths can be harnessed to teach skills, provide meaningful practice opportunities, and promote on-task behavior. Confidence, motivation, active participation, and academic progress often increase when activities match student strengths. Thus, incorporating strengths will increase learning and allow the student to move more successfully across their multiple environments.

Autistic strengths include the following:

- Thrives in structure
- Pays attention to detail
- Likes order
- Is punctual
- Has good rote memory
- Is a good greeter
- Is a loyal friend
- Wants to have friends
- Is a logical thinker
- Is motivated by special interests
- Has a sense of social justice
- Wants to be independent
- Is creative
- Is highly motivated to complete activities in areas of interest
- Follows rules when they are taught and practiced
- Does well when breaks are provided throughout the day
- Performs better when prepared in advance using visuals
- Learns well when visual instruction is provided
- Responds well to positive reinforcement
- Does well when time and problems to complete match
- Transitions well with a visual support and advance warning
- Has sensory-related skills, such as perfect pitch, identifying smells and/or sounds that are mixed together, and strong visual search skills

### *Challenges*

*Challenges* in this context refer to skills and behaviors that require instruction and support. Incorporating challenges as instructional goals and essential supports on the student's IEP can decrease the mismatch between the student's skills and the environment, thus increasing student success. Addressing challenges increases instructional time, student independence, and academic performance. Concurrently, the frequency and severity of meltdowns decrease.

Skills that require instruction and support—often called challenges—include the following:

- Expressing wants and needs by raising voice
- Inherently knowing how to make and keep friends
- Hyper- or hypo-sensory responses
- Concrete learner
- Knowledge of emotional vocabulary
- Interoception
- Understanding the social world
- Understanding unstated rules
- Following verbal direction and routines
- Problem-solving
- Conflict resolution
- Compromising
- Prediction
- Organizing desk, locker, and self
- Understanding different contexts
- Adjusting to change
- Executive function
- Gross-motor skills

- Dysregulation when unprepared for an activity
- Interacting with others and meeting academic demands in less structured settings

### *Things That Upset*

Many autistics experience regulation challenges because their brains are not wired to automatically know how to match their emotions to the environment. To further complicate matters, many have difficulty detecting how they are feeling without direct instruction.

Regulation for autistic students is an instructional issue, and it often takes a significant amount of time to learn and practice this skill. As a result, it is essential that educators understand their student's regulation system so they intervene early to support the student to calm down.

Parents, who have the most information about their child's regulation skills, can help educators understand what events may prompt dysregulation. Examples include the following:

- Sensory violations
- Changes
- Not being prepared for changes
- Transitions
- Someone standing too close
- Not knowing what to do
- Not being able to see the clock
- Being ignored
- The color yellow
- New environments
- Uncertainty
- Too many people
- Not knowing the schedule
- Surprises
- Sudden, loud noises
- Being late
- Small talk
- Someone who breaks the rules

### *Signs of Being Upset*

For those who experience regulation challenges, minor behaviors can quickly escalate to meltdowns. As mentioned, dysregulation in autistics signals a need for instruction and support. Behaviors that indicate dysregulation are not purposeful behaviors—again, they indicate a need for instruction and support.

Autistic individuals exhibit specific behavioral changes that indicate dysregulation. They may bite their nails or lips, lower their voices, tense their muscles, grimace, or otherwise indicate general discontent. In addition, they may appear to be slightly off task, disengaged, or off the mark. They may complain of not feeling well. In other instances, autistic individuals engage in behaviors that are more pronounced, including withdrawing from others, either emotionally or physically; threatening others, either verbally or physically; or questioning the rules or authority.

The following are examples of behaviors that may signal that the student is dysregulated:

- Fidgeting
- Swearing
- Making noises
- Ripping paper
- Grimacing
- Putting head on desk
- Picking at nails
- Rocking
- Chewing on collar/cuffs
- Throwing objects
- Refusing to cooperate
- Rapid movements
- Tears
- Name-calling
- Changed voice volume
- Tapping foot
- Negative talk

It is easy to ignore these seemingly minor behaviors, yet they often signal the beginning of the cycle of meltdowns and, therefore, require monitoring and attention (see Myles 2024 for additional information).

### *Calming Strategies*

Just as autistics often do not implicitly recognize the causes of their dysregulation or their dysregulation behaviors, many do not know what actions to take when they need to calm down. Thus, they need direct instruction, support, and coaching and multiple practice opportunities to use calming strategies.

Parents who share information about their child's calming skills and needs help teachers provide interventions and supports that build on the student's existing skills. Parents may report using a variety of calming strategies, including the following:

- Break area/home base
- Distractions
- Exercise and routine
- Meditation/mindfulness strategies
- Music
- Provide space
- Limiting the words used when the child is upset
- Apps, such as Calm, Headspace, and Breathe2Relax
- Album of calming pictures
- Movement and exercise
- Four-square breathing or other breathing routine
- Drawing/coloring
- Sensory items (e.g., weighted vests, lap pads, swing, weighted blanket, fidgets, chew, glitter bottle, galactic sphere)

Teachers may need to ask parents follow-up questions in order to understand how to use the regulation strategies they report. For example, if the child uses their bedroom as a home base, it can be helpful if parents can answer the following questions in detail:

1. How do you let your child know that it is time for them to go calm down?
2. How do you direct your child to the bedroom? What does this look like? Does this always work?
3. Is there a specific part of the bedroom the child uses to calm?
4. What does the child do when they go to the bedroom?
5. Does your child need help to calm once in the bedroom?
6. How long does it take your child to get calm?

### *Necessary Supports*

Some students require specific supports in order to thrive; without them, daily activities often lead to frustration and a sense of failure. When identifying necessary supports, it is helpful to think in terms of unfamiliar and familiar activities. Often a high level of support is needed in new activities. As the student becomes comfortable with the routine, supports may be modified or lessened. Nevertheless, many autistics have an ongoing need for supports.

Some of the following may be necessary to support a student in a novel activity; some may be required for ongoing support:

- Prepare for activities
- Visual schedule for the day
- Mini-schedule of activities, such as brushing teeth
- Break room/home base
- Travel bag of supports
- Downtime
- Frequent reinforcement
- Spinning wheel of choices of activities with friends
- Short, structured social activities
- Sensory basket
- Calming classical music playing
- Student moving at their own pace without being rushed
- Verbal prompts to stay on task
- Time with special interest
- Five-minute alert before an activity begins/ends

## Completion of the Learner Snapshot

While parents can complete the Learner Snapshot using paper/pencil or computer, the preferred way of obtaining the information is through an interview. During the interview, the child's teacher learns about the student, and the teacher and parent begin to develop a relationship focused on the child's success.

It is often beneficial to include the student in completing the Learner Snapshot. The student can offer valuable insights into (a) their understanding of their learning profile, including strengths, concerns, and skills, and (b) their understanding of interventions that have been implemented and their effectiveness.

## Summary

The more information a teacher knows about a student, the more successful the teacher will be in developing and implementing a program that will help the student have a successful school experience. The Learner Snapshot, a parent interview, is designed to quickly identify salient details about the student that can be incorporated into lessons, reinforcement systems, and relationship development.

# Chapter 3

## Learner Snapshot

*Brenda Smith Myles and Judy Marks*

**Directions to parents:** This interview is designed to help your child's teachers better understand your child. The information you are comfortable sharing will be used in planning your child's schedule, interventions, and supports. As such, it will provide insights that will support your child's learning while minimizing discomfort as they transition.

**Learner Name:** ______________________ **Date:** ______________________

**Completed by:** ______________________

| Exceptionality Description |
| --- |
| |

| Family Description |
| --- |
| |

| Learns Best |
| --- |
| |

| Special Interests/Preferences/Motivators |
| --- |
| |

| Strengths |
| --- |
| |

| Challenges |
| --- |
| |

| Things That Upset |
| --- |
| |

| Signs of Being Upset |
| --- |
| |

| Effective Ways to Help Your Child Calm Down |
| --- |
| |

| Necessary Supports to Ensure Success at Home, School, and Community |
| --- |
| |

# PART III

## If Difficulties Occur

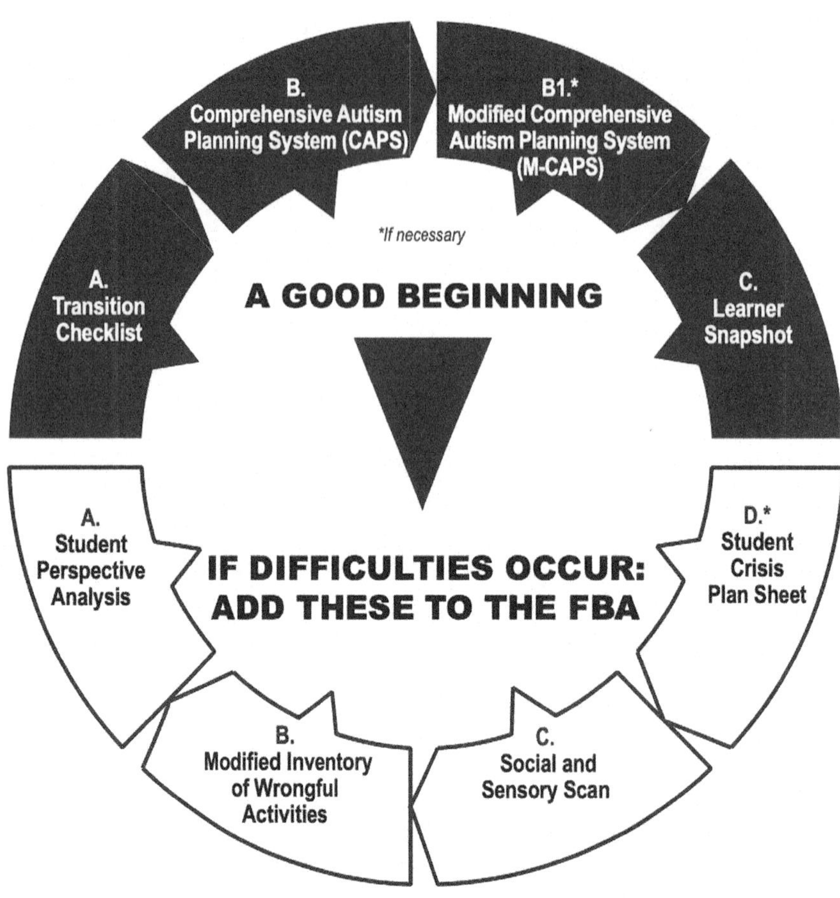


Part III of this book provides information on how to support a student who is experiencing challenges at school. Because autistic students have neurologically-based regulation challenges, meltdowns are often a concern. We suggest that educators add three measures to their typical functional behavior assessment (FBA) and behavior implementation process (BIP).

To that end, we introduce to the Student Perspective Analysis, the Modified Inventory of Wrong Activities, and the Social and Sensory Scan worksheet to help educators better understand the student in crisis. Once FBA and the three additional measures are completed and analyzed, the BIP, required by law, is developed. The information on the BIP is synthesized on the Student Crisis Plan (see below), a user-friendly form that guides educators through how to support the student who is experiencing a meltdown.

- **Student Perspective Analysis (grades 4–12).** This student interview asks specific questions about each class and teacher such as, "Is the work difficult or easy?," "If you could change one thing about [name the teacher], what would you change?," and "Which students do you have a problem with?" This tool gives insight into how the student thinks about school.

- **Modified Inventory of Wrongful Activities (grades 4–12).** Recognizing that most autistics are bullied in school, this student interview covers the various types of bullying using easy-to-understand terms: verbal, social, electronic, and education (Heinrichs 2003). This tool can be completed by the student individually with a follow-up interview or through a stand-alone interview. Students need protection from bullying, and this tool is invaluable in identifying when, where, and from whom the student needs protection.

- **The Social and Sensory Scan (grades 4–12).** A trusted adult assists the student in scanning environments that do not match their needs (Paradiz 2009). Mismatches often result in the student becoming dysregulated. This instrument provides the student's perspective on their multiple environments—an important view that is often neglected. Results of completing this scan can (a) help educators modify environments for student success and (b) serve as a blueprint for teaching students to recognize their social and sensory needs and implement supports.

- **Student Crisis Plan Sheet (K–12).** The school team completes this brief instrument when developing the student's behavior intervention plan (BIP). The Student Crisis Plan Sheet provides a blueprint for how to support the student during the cycle of meltdowns. This brief and easy-to-complete form synthesizes the student's BIP into a series of indicators and interventions.

The following chapters describe the instruments and how they are administered.

# Chapter 4

## Student Perspective Analysis

To most effectively and efficiently support a student who is dysregulated, it is important to understand why the dysregulation is occurring. That is, we need to understand the causes or functions of that student's behavior. The goal is not simply to eradicate the dysregulating behavior, but to help the student learn new and more appropriate ways of getting their needs met. Understanding the why is one of the initial steps in setting up an effective intervention.

Instruction and support are the best ways to ensure that the student does not encounter challenging situations without the appropriate skills and supports.

Dysregulated behavior is complex and occurs for a variety of reasons. Identifying the reasons behind it can be helpful in identifying needed instruction and support. The following is a nonexhaustive list of reasons why dysregulation occurs:

- Needs instruction on the many ways of understanding or knowing what to do
- Requires instruction on strategies, other than escape or avoid, to use when confronted with difficult situations
- Needs instruction and support on how to gain positive attention from peers and adults
- Because of challenges recognizing their feelings (e.g., anger, stress, frustration) and pain or discomfort (e.g., sinus pain, skin irritation, hunger, needing to go to the bathroom); requires instruction to understand their interoception system
- Needs instruction and coaching to identify supportive people and ask for support
- Because of difficulty recognizing sensory under- or over-reactivity in self; requires instruction in identifying needs and seeking supports that make the environment more compatible with student's autism
- Requires instruction on how organize their environments, such as knowing how to organize items in their desk and when to throw something away
- Needs to learn multiple strategies that match their many environments to get needs met (e.g., how to obtain activity or follow a routine object at recess, in the hallway, in the lunchroom, during a lecture)

- Needs strategies to recognize and react in a productive manner to fears related to (a) failure, (b) self-esteem (e.g., embarrassment, loss of perceived position), (c) objects, (d) people, (e) events, and so on
- Needs instruction in when and how to defend a personal idea, opinion, or thought across environments and various individuals

Clearly, dysregulation occurs because the student's needs and the environment do not match. As a result, student responses should be viewed through this lens. That is, when developing a school program, it is essential that the school team, including parents, integrate instruction, supports, coaching, and multiple practice opportunities to help change unproductive perspectives to more helpful and pragmatic ones.

## Description

The Student Perspective Analysis (SPA) can be helpful in understanding how the student perceives the school day. That is, items are intended to elicit the student's likes and dislikes related to peers, teachers, and social and academic demands as well as to provide information on each of his classes. The interview is best used when the student is experiencing challenging behavior to determine if bullying is related to their behavior. A description of its components follows.

### *School*

The student is asked twenty-nine questions about each of their classes. Questions begin with seemingly basic information—asking the student to name the class and teacher. It is essential that the interviewer have the student's schedule readily available, as they may not readily recall this information. Questions are designed to ascertain information on the following:

- **The teacher-student relationship**, such as how the teacher reinforces the student and whether the teacher does anything to "bother" the student
- **Activities and the student's perspective of them**, such as group and individual group, if the work is easy or difficult, whether the student feels skilled in the subject area, homework requirements
- **Time constraints**, including whether adequate time to complete assignments and transition is provided
- **Classroom structure**, such as physical set-up and routines

Students are then asked to rank their classes and teachers from best to worst. This information is not meant to evaluate teacher performance. Rather, the rankings allow a comparison of student perspectives with student academic and nonacademic behaviors.

### *Bus*

Many aspects of getting to and from school by bus must be carefully considered to determine if the student needs supports to ensure an uneventful, safe ride for everyone. Questions in this section of the SPA address the following:

- **The bus driver-student relationship**, such as whether the student knows the bus driver's name and whether the student perceives that the bus driver likes them;
- **Social interactions**, including whether there are peers on the bus that the student likes, who sits by the student, whether the student and peers interact with each other, and what these interactions look like.

### *Lunch*

For most students, lunch is a time to relax, recharge, and visit with friends. But for many autistic students, it is just the opposite—a time to (a) perform untaught routines, (b) rush, (c) experience sensory overstimulation, (d) encounter unsatisfactory food choices, and (e) face peer rejection and even bullying. Keeping this in mind, the SPA includes questions that address lunch issues, such as time, noise, smells, and social interactions, that often require support.

## Completion of the Student Perspective Analysis

The SPA is designed as an interview. Additional materials, such as the student's daily schedule, are required for administration. Some students may need to see teacher names in written and/or pictorial format as well as class names to prompt responses because they do not know the names of their teacher(s) even after several months. The interviewer should also be prepared with the names, photos, and roles of other adults (e.g., lunch personnel, bus driver) the student regularly comes in contact with. For students who process information visually, providing them with a copy of the interview can promote understanding and on-task behavior.

As the student will be asked about each of their teachers, interviewers are asked to directly insert the names of teachers and class names into relevant questions. Using names and avoiding pronouns makes questions easier to understand (see examples below).

The questions are designed with literal learners in mind, using direct statements so students do not need to make inferences. Even then, some students may misunderstand questions or respond literally, so interviewers may need to reword some items. Despite these limitations, the SPA can provide information that directly translates into instruction and supports for the student. Examples of student responses on the SPA show their importance for gaining an insight into the student's perceptions and, therefore, developing appropriate supports and interventions.

**Examples of SPA Questions and Student Responses**

| SPA Question | Student Response |
|---|---|
| Does [teacher name] like you? | I heard she wants me out of her class. Does that count? |
| How does [teacher name] let you know what the homework is? | He writes it on the board. Sometimes in red. It's hard to read it when it is in red or yellow. |
| Did you tell him? | I don't want to tell him because the other kids might laugh at me. |
| Does [teacher name] make any changes that bother you? | She lies all the time. Yesterday she said we were going to have homework and we didn't. |
| Do you have time to switch activities in [class name]? | Not when I'm not finished. He [the teacher] can see that I'm not done, and he makes us switch anyway! |

*FIGURE 4.1*

## Summary

The SPA offers a way to understand how the student views the school day. Often administered over several days, this instrument asks questions about the academic and nonacademic classes, teachers, and peers to develop a comprehensive picture of how the student moves throughout the school day.

# Student Perspective Analysis (SPA)

| **Student name:** | **Date:** |
|---|---|

**Who administered SPA :**

**Directions for the Interviewer:**

When preparing for the interview, be aware that the SPA may need to be administered across several sessions. Gather as much information as possible beforehand. Helpful information may include the following:

- The student's daily schedule
- Teachers' names/photos and the courses they teach
- Names and roles of other adults the student encounters
- Recent classroom assignments in all subject areas

Discuss with the student the reason for gathering information. The following script can be used to help the student understand the interview:

The reason I'm asking these questions is so we can learn about the things that are bothering you at school. Some of these things we may be able to fix. Other things we cannot change.

> *Just because I'm listening to your answers does not mean that I can change all of these things. It may be helpful for your teachers to know this information so they may better understand you. When a person learns what is on someone's mind, it provides information about what someone is thinking. This can help people get along and respect each other, even if many things about the situation cannot be changed.*

When asking questions, it is essential to name the school subject or the name of a teacher, rather than using pronouns. Because pronouns can be confusing, the questions will be clearer if you specifically use the teacher's name, rather than *he*, *she*, or *they*.

**SCHOOL** *(Questions 1–29 should be answered for each class.)*

| Question | Student Response |
|---|---|
| 1. What is your first (next) class in school? | |
| 2. Who's your teacher? | |
| 3. Does teacher's name notice when you do a good job? | |
| 4. What does teacher's name do that tells you you've done a good job? | |
| 5. Do you think teacher's name likes you? | |

| | |
|---|---|
| 6. What does teacher's name do to show you they like you? | |
| 7. Do you usually work alone or with others? | |
| 8. What kinds of things do you do alone? | |
| 9. What kinds of things do you do with others? | |
| 10. Which do you prefer? | |
| 11. Is the work difficult or easy? | |
| 12. What is the easy part of the schoolwork? | |
| 13. What part of schoolwork don't you like in name class or subject? | |
| 14. If you could change one thing about name class/subject, what would that be? | |
| 15. Name one easy thing in subject name class. | |
| 16. What is one thing you are good at in subject's name class? | |
| 17. Do you have any problems with other students in teacher's name class? | |
| 18. Which students do you have problems with? | |
| 19. Tell me about the problem(s)? | |
| 20. What would help the situation? | |
| 21. Do you always sit in the same seat? | |
| 22. Do you like where you are sitting? Why or why not? | |
| 23. How does teacher's name let you know what the homework is? | |

| | |
|---|---|
| 24. Does teacher's name make any changes that bother you? | |
| 25. Can you think of anything teacher's name does that bothers you? What? | |
| 26. Are there any things in the classroom that really bother you a lot? (noises, smell, light, temperature, etc.) | |
| 27. Do you have enough time to do what teacher's name asks? | |
| 28. Do you have enough time to switch activities in name the class? | |
| 29. Do you have enough time to get your work done? | |

30. Rank your classes (including bus, lunch) in order, with 1 being the best and __ being the worst. (Give the student a list of all classes and activities.)

| Rank | Classes |
|---|---|
| | |
| | |
| | |
| | |
| | |
| | |
| | |
| | |
| | |
| | |

31. Rank your teachers and other adults you see at school in order, with 1 being the best and __ being the worst. (Give the student list of teachers and adults to include.)

| Rank | Classes |
|---|---|
| | |
| | |
| | |
| | |
| | |
| | |
| | |
| | |
| | |
| | |

**BUS** *(You may need to conduct two interviews: one for the morning bus and another for the afternoon bus.)*

| | |
|---|---|
| 32. Who is your bus driver? | |
| 33. Does bus driver's name like you? Dislike you? | |
| 34. What does the bus driver do that tells you that the bus driver likes/doesn't like you? | |
| 35. Do you sit in the same seat every day? | |
| 36. Does anyone sit in the seat next to you? Who? | |
| 37. Are there students on your bus you like? Who? | |
| 38. Do you ever talk to them? | |
| 39. What do you talk about? | |
| 40. What do they talk about? | |

# Student Perspective Analysis (SPA)

| | |
|---|---|
| 41. Are there students on the bus you do not like? Who? | |
| 42. Why don't you like them? | |
| 43. Do you like riding the bus? Why or why not? (If no, question further.) | |

**LUNCH**

| | |
|---|---|
| 44. What time do you eat lunch? | |
| 45. Do you always sit in the same seat? | |
| 46. Who do you like to sit with at lunch? | |
| 47. Is there anyone you do not like to sit with at lunch? Who? Why? | |
| 48. Do you have enough time to eat lunch? | |
| 49. Do you like lunchtime? | |
| 50. Does the noise in the cafeteria bother you? | |
| 51. Do the smells in the cafeteria bother you? | |
| 52. If you could change one thing about lunch time, what would it be? | |

# Chapter 5

## Modified Inventory of Wrongful Activities

Approximately two-thirds of autistic students are bullied (Hwang et al. 2018; Park 2020), and the impact of bullying is both long-term and devastating. Students who are bullied can end up becoming long-lasting victims of fear, anxiety, physical illness, and depression. Recent research has shown that bullied students show chemical changes in their brains that can lead to (a) lessened ability to self-regulate and (b) psychosis (Okada et al. 2024).

The Modified Inventory of Wrongful Activities (MIWA; Heinrichs, n.d.) was developed to assist autistic students in identifying whether they are victims of bullying. Adapted from Brown's (n.d.) Inventory of Wrongful Activities (http://www.safeculture.com/iowa.html), questions and responses are stated concisely, and examples are typically given when social language or nonverbal communication is involved.

### Description

The MIWA uniquely addresses the various types of bullying:

- **Physical bullying:** Includes hitting; pushing; tripping; kicking; spitting on someone; pulling hair; shouldering; grabbing clothes, belongings, or parts of a person's body; and any other types of hands-on physical actions

- **Verbal bullying:** Includes teasing and making fun of someone, verbal threats, name-calling, and other types of incidents involving language. Some verbal bullying includes obscene gestures, eye-rolling, threatening stares, or other types of nonverbal communication because it is a representation of words.

- **Social bullying:** Occurs when the intent is to isolate or exclude someone from peers by spreading rumors, peer shunning, humiliation, or other methods of damaging or manipulating relationships.

- **Educational bullying:** Occurs when adults who perform as members of the school team use their power to either intentionally or unintentionally harm students, causing them distress. This may include the use of sarcasm, being overly critical and controlling, humiliating students in front of their peers, favoring students, and being overly punitive (Heinrichs 2003).

In addition, students are asked (a) when and where bullying occurs, (b) what adults do when they become aware of bullying, and (c) which adults are likely to support the bullied student.

A sample item of the MIWA illustrates the level of specificity recommended. "Used hand signals to be mean (like making an *L* with their fingers and putting it on their forehead)" or "Insulted me with sexual talk or jokes (could include hand signals like raising the middle finger or name-calling like 'slut' or 'fag')." This questionnaire is probably best suited for older elementary, middle, and high schoolers. Even though some of the language may seem harsh, it is a mistake to shy away from gathering this type of sensitive information, because it reflects an unfortunate reality for students in our schools.

## Completion of the Modified Inventory of Wrongful Activities

This measure is best suited for older elementary, middle, and high schoolers. It can be administered as a survey or interview. If the student completes the survey independently, it is essential that a trusted adult conducts an individual *interview* with them as well. That is, after the autistic student completes the survey, an individual interview using the survey as a guide will help ensure a more complete picture of their social lives.

## Summary

Bullying is prevalent in schools, and autistic students are particularly prone to being bullied because of the way they understand and interact in their environment. Sadly, bullying has long-term outcomes impacting the mental health of students in adulthood. The MIWA can help adults better understand the bullying that occurs under their supervision so that an effective plan to protect and support the student can be developed and put in place.

# Chapter 5

## Modified Inventory of Wrongful Activities (MIWA)

*Rebekah Heinrichs*

Has a student (or students) from your school done any of the following things to you? CHECK ALL ITEMS that have happened to you THIS SCHOOL YEAR.

**SOMEONE HAS:**

- ☐ 1. Pulled my hair, hit, pinched, kicked, tripped, bit, or spit on me
- ☐ 2. Torn my clothes or broken my things (such as pencil breaking)
- ☐ 3. Stolen from me
- ☐ 4. Scared me or threatened me with a weapon (like a knife or gun)

**SOMEONE HAS:**

- ☐ 5. Said bad things about me (calling me names like "fat" or "freak")
- ☐ 6. Said bad things about my family (like calling my dad a "wimp")
- ☐ 7. Written mean notes about me
- ☐ 8. Made me afraid to talk in class or make mistakes because of teasing
- ☐ 9. Asked me to do things that I get in trouble for doing (like saying something rude to the teacher)
- ☐ 10. Scared or threatened me into doing something I didn't want to do (like giving up money or doing someone else's homework)
- ☐ 11. Asked me to do things that make me uncomfortable (like telling me not to talk to certain people)
- ☐ 12. Made it hard for me to learn in school because I feel scared, angry, sad, or upset about the way people treat me
- ☐ 13. Made me not want to go to school because I feel scared, angry, sad, or upset about the way people treat me
- ☐ 14. Left me out of a group or activity
- ☐ 15. Made mean faces at me (like rolling eyes)
- ☐ 16. Laughed at me to be mean

Modified by Rebekah Heinrichs from the original Inventory of Wrongful Activities written by Dennis Brown, safeculture.com, Safe Culture© Project DB (n.d.).

**SOMEONE HAS:**

- ❑ 17. Used hand signals to be mean (like making an L with their fingers and putting it on their forehead)
- ❑ 18. Made fun of something they think is different about me (like being tall or short, wearing glasses or braces, or talking or walking differently)
- ❑ 19. Insulted me because I am in a different class or program
- ❑ 20. Insulted me or made jokes about my color or race
- ❑ 21. Insulted my ability to learn in class
- ❑ 22. Made fun of my clothes or my parents' car, house, or job
- ❑ 23. Insulted me with sexual talk or jokes (could include hand signals like raising the middle finger or name-calling like "slut" or "fag")
- ❑ 24. Spread sexual rumors about me (like telling people I am "gay" or "easy")
- ❑ 25. Made me uncomfortable by taking off their clothes or mooning me (*Mooning* is when someone exposes their bare buttocks to another.)
- ❑ 26. Pulled (or tried to pull) my clothes off or down
- ❑ 27. Touched, grabbed, pinched, or kicked me in a private area
- ❑ 28. Touched me in a sexual way without my permission (like kissing, hugging, putting hands on my private areas or holding me)
- ❑ 29. Written sexual insults about me on walls, desks, or something else

The next three statements ask for your feelings about your teachers and their actions. CHECK ALL ITEMS that are TRUE for you.

- ❑ 30. I feel some teachers don't like me as well as they like other students.
- ❑ 31. I feel hurt or angry (once a week or more) about a teacher's actions or words.
- ❑ 32. I wish my teachers would stop someone who is acting mean to me.

Modified by Rebekah Heinrichs from the original Inventory of Wrongful Activities written by Dennis Brown, safeculture.com, Safe Culture© Project DB (n.d.).

The next three statements ask for your feelings about your teachers and their actions. CHECK ALL ITEMS that are TRUE for you.

**When are mean things said or done to you?**

☐ 33. Before school

☐ 34. Between classes

☐ 35. After school

☐ 36. During classes

☐ 37. At lunchtime

☐ 38. At after-school activities

**What places should adults watch better to keep students from being mean to you?**

☐ 39. Hallways

☐ 40. Bathrooms

☐ 41. Classrooms

☐ 42. Lunchroom

☐ 43. Gym lockers

☐ 44. Outside on school property

**Choose ONLY ONE answer for the next eight questions and WRITE THE LETTER on the line provided.**

__ 45. Do people act mean to you on the school bus?
A. I do not ride the school bus.
B. People **do not** act mean to me on the school bus I ride.
C. People **do** act mean to me on the school bus I ride.

__ 46. What do most of your teachers do when they see students acting mean?
A. They usually do nothing. They ignore it.
B. They do very little. They might say, "Quit that."
C. They make them stop and teach them not to act that way anymore.

__ 47. What do you do when you see students acting mean to other students?
A. I sometimes join in and act mean too.
B. I do nothing. I ignore it.
C. I ask people to stop acting mean. I try to stop it.
D. I tell a teacher so he or she can help.

Modified by Rebekah Heinrichs from the original Inventory of Wrongful Activities written by Dennis Brown, safeculture.com, Safe Culture© Project DB (n.d.).

___ 48. What do you do when people are mean to you at school?
- A. I act mean right back.
- B. I do nothing. I ignore it or accept it.
- C. I tell them to stop.
- D. I tell a teacher so he or she can help.

___ 49. How often are people mean to you at school?
- A. Almost never
- B. Several times a week
- C. About once a day
- D. More than once a day

___ 50. How often do you tell adults at school when people are mean to you?
- A. I almost never tell.
- B. I tell some of the time.
- C. I tell most of the time.
- D. I tell every time.

___ 51. What usually happens when you tell an adult at school about someone being mean to you?
- A. It helps a lot
- B. It helps some
- C. It does not make a difference
- D. It makes things worse

___ 52. What usually happens when you tell your parents about someone being mean to you?
- A. It helps a lot
- B. It helps some
- C. It does not make a difference
- D. It makes things worse

CHECK ALL ITEMS that are TRUE for you. Which adults at school do you go to for help when someone is being mean to you?

- ☐ 53. Counselor
- ☐ 54. Teacher
- ☐ 55. School psychologist
- ☐ 56. Principal
- ☐ 57. Vice/assistant principal
- ☐ 58. Resource teacher
- ☐ 59. Paraprofessional/aide
- ☐ 60. Resource police officer
- ☐ 61. Other (please specify) ______________________________

Modified by Rebekah Heinrichs from the original Inventory of Wrongful Activities written by Dennis Brown, safeculture.com, Safe Culture© Project DB (n.d.).

Please include any additional comments here:

Modified by Rebekah Heinrichs from the original Inventory of Wrongful Activities written by Dennis Brown, safeculture.com, Safe Culture© Project DB (n.d.).

# Chapter 6

## Social and Sensory Scan

Many autistic people experience the world differently from their neuromajority peers, especially in the social and sensory areas. Strong evidence, both from a behavioral and a neurobiological standpoint, suggests that the autistic brain requires a variety of supports as well as direct instruction, coaching, and multiple practice opportunities in order to arrive at a match between themselves and the environment (cf. Gara et al. 2020).

When students are in crisis, the school team understands that as they conduct a functional behavior assessment (FBA), it is important to look at the behavior through multiple perspectives, including through a social and sensory lens. Often, responses from the FBA, combined with those from the Student Perspective Analysis (SPA), reveal that additional information is needed. The Modified Sensory and Social Scan can be helpful in this regard.

### Description

The Social and Sensory Scan is based on Valerie Paradiz's (2009) *Integrated Self-Advocacy Curriculum (ISA): A Program for Emerging Self-Advocates with Autism Spectrum and Other Conditions*. The purposes of the book are best paraphrased from its introduction:

**To autistics:** When I say that I wrote this book for *you*, I really mean it. The activities in this book are meant to make you feel at home with autism and with yourself. So, I ask you to keep one thing in mind as you discover the joys of self-advocacy. As teachers, therapists, and support people, we are learning right along with you. In fact, as you'll see, the more you can discover about yourself on this journey, the more you'll enrich their lives, too!

**To teachers, professionals, doctors, therapists, case managers, our families, and others who support us:** I wrote this book for you because I want you to know that we autistics are self-aware beings, and we can become more self-aware and can advocate for what we need to be happy when we are given the tools, respect, and permission to do so.

Specifically, Paradiz's book helps learners do the following:

- Understand autism in the context of its (a) characteristics, (b) history, and (c) role models in the autism community
- Recognize the impact of the media on how others understand autism
- Understand their individual strengths and needs
- Develop a self-advocacy plan
- Understand and become a part of other aspects of self-advocacy, such as IEP and American Disabilities Act (ADA) activities
- Identify and describe environmental elements (e.g., lighting, handwriting, verbal instruction, visual schedules) that support their learning and interactions
- Describe how these elements can lead to success using a self-advocacy script
- Conduct an analysis of their environments using The Sensory Scan and The Social Scan
- Identify and advocate for needed instruction, coaching, practice, and supports

The Social and Sensory Scan presented here was developed using Paradiz's two tools. Specifically, the two were combined recognizing that both aspects of the environment—social and sensory—could be assessed during one session. For the present purposes, similar items across the two measures were combined and some wording was altered to reflect current trends and perspectives in the world of autism.

| Areas Addressed on the Social and Sensory Scan | |
|---|---|
| **Social** | **Sensory** |
| People | Sound |
| Space | Vision |
| Activity | Smell |
| Expectations | Touch/Feel |
| Mood | Taste |
| Helpful Supports | Movement and Space |
| | Sensory Challenges |

*FIGURE 6.1*

A sincere attempt has been made to be true to Valerie Paradiz's intent. With sincere apologies, Valerie. Additional information may be found in *The Integrated Self-Advocacy (ISA) Curriculum: A Program for Emerging Self-Advocates with Autism Spectrum and Other Conditions* (Paradiz 2009).

##  Completion of the Social and Sensory Scan

Because we suggest that the Social and Sensory Scan be used when it becomes apparent that the student needs additional (or different) instruction and supports, it is likely that the student is dysregulated. Even if the student does not appear to be dysregulated at the moment, they have experienced repeated bouts of dysregulation in the recent past. ... And they are likely to occur again, unless the student's program changes. So consider the student dysregulated. And because dysregulation is often accompanied by decreased academic and executive function performance, assume that the student cannot accurately complete the scale independently. To complete the scan, the student will need to do the following:

- Be taught the purpose of the instrument and how to complete it.
- Practice, perhaps more than once, completing the instrument with a trusted support person.
- Be prepared in advance or primed to enter the designated environments with the trusted support person. This includes knowing when to enter, where to sit with space for the support person next to the student, whether the adult or student will write responses, what type of prompts or redirection will be used, and under what circumstances they will be used.
- Be supported during the completion of the Social and Sensory Scan consistent with information shared during the priming session.

##  Summary

The Social and Sensory Scan taps into the student's perspective of their environment. Simply-worded questions help to identify potential areas of concern that can be addressed through instruction and/or support. The tool is helpful when the student experiences dysregulation. It can also be preemptive. That is, the student can also be taught to use this tool proactively to better understand novel environments. Further, the scan can be used across the lifespan to scan environments, including (a) postsecondary education/training situations, (b) employment sites, (c) a vacation rental location, and (d) the homes of friends.

## The Social and Sensory Scan

This instrument can be completed by the well-regulated student who can understand its content. If this occurs, an individual interview must be conducted to clarify or seek additional information. The instrument can also be used as an interview administered by a trusted support person.

**Name:** ______________________ **Setting:** ______________________

**Date:** ______________________ **Interviewer:** ______________________

### The Social Environment

1. **PEOPLE:** Look at **the people** in this setting. Answer these questions. Fill in as many details as you can.

   About how many people are here? ____________

   About how many of the people here do you **know**? ____________

My comfort level with people in this setting is (circle one):

unbearable        uncomfortable        not a problem        comfortable

2. **SPACE:** Look **around you** to answer the following questions.

   What does the space **look like**? (check all that apply)

   - ❑ People are seated in rows of chairs or at table(s) or desk(s) for a lecture.
   - ❑ People are standing/sitting in groups, and they might move around.
   - ❑ People are working by themselves.

   Please describe the space:

   ______________________________________________

   ______________________________________________

   Is there **enough space** for you? (check all that apply)

   - ❑ Yes, there is enough space.
   - ❑ No, there are too many things (like desks, equipment, or supplies) here.
   - ❑ Yes, there is about the right number of people.
   - ❑ No, people are too close to me.
   - ❑ Other (please describe):

   ______________________________________________

   ______________________________________________

Modified from Paradiz, V. (2009). *The Integrated Self-Advocacy ISA™ Curriculum—A Program for Emerging Self-Advocates with Autism Spectrum and Other Conditions.* Lenexa, KS: Autism Asperger Publishing Company (2009). Out of print.

Is there **anything in the space** that helps you understand what to do?

- ❑ There are pictures, signs, lists, schedules, or other symbols that help me understand.
- ❑ The way people are sitting or standing or are organized helps me understand what to do.
- ❑ I am not sure if there is anything here that helps me know what to do.
- ❑ Other (please describe):

______________________________________________

______________________________________________

My comfort level with the setting is (circle one):

unbearable    uncomfortable    not a problem    comfortable

3. **ACTIVITY:** What is the topic today (such as multiplying by 10, adverbs, the causes of the Revolutionary War)?

______________________________________________

My comfort level with the setting is (circle one):

unbearable    uncomfortable    not a problem    comfortable

4. **EXPECTATIONS:** Think about **what you are supposed to be doing** in this environment.

- ❑ I am expected to participate with others in an activity.
- ❑ I can participate if I want, but I do not have to.
- ❑ I am not sure what to do.
- ❑ I am expected to be quiet and listen.
- ❑ I can use a fidget.
- ❑ I can get up and move around if I need to.
- ❑ I can ask for help and get it without getting into trouble.
- ❑ Other (please describe):

______________________________________________

______________________________________________

My comfort level with the expectations in this setting is (circle one):

unbearable    uncomfortable    not a problem    comfortable

Modified from Paradiz, V. (2009). *The Integrated Self-Advocacy ISA™ Curriculum—A Program for Emerging Self-Advocates with Autism Spectrum and Other Conditions.* Lenexa, KS: Autism Asperger Publishing Company (2009). Out of print.

5. **MOOD:** What is the **mood or the emotions of others** in this setting?

- ❑ The mood is happy.
- ❑ The mood is sad.
- ❑ The mood is focused. People are concentrating on something or someone.
- ❑ The mood is angry. If yes, who is angry? ____________________
- ❑ I am not sure what the mood is.
- ❑ Other (please describe):

____________________

My comfort level with the mood or emotions of others in this setting is (circle one):

unbearable uncomfortable not a problem comfortable

6. **OTHER INFORMATION:** What parts of the environment (such as the people, the work, the space, how you know what to do) are helpful to you? Please describe:

____________________

____________________

## The Sensory Environment

1. **SOUND**: Pay attention to **the sounds** in this environment (check all that apply).

- ❑ The sound is okay for me.
- ❑ There are sudden loud noises.
- ❑ Too many people are talking at one time.
- ❑ Background noise is distracting.
- ❑ Voices are too loud.
- ❑ I need headphones or earbuds.
- ❑ Other (please describe): ____________________

2. **VISION**: Pay attention to **what you see or how you see** in this setting (check all that apply).

- ❑ Light in room is too bright or too dim.
- ❑ Angle of light is difficult (from above, below, etc.).
- ❑ Signs and schedules are easy to read.
- ❑ Type of light is hard for me to see in.
- ❑ I can read the board easily.
- ❑ There is too much on walls or hanging from the ceiling.
- ❑ Other (please describe): ____________________

Modified from Paradiz, V. (2009). *The Integrated Self-Advocacy ISA™ Curriculum—A Program for Emerging Self-Advocates with Autism Spectrum and Other Conditions.* Lenexa, KS: Autism Asperger Publishing Company (2009). Out of print.

3. **SMELL**: Pay attention to the **smells** in this environment (check all that apply).

   - ❑ Smell from objects is distracting, challenging.
   - ❑ General smell of the room is hard to stand.
   - ❑ Smell from person(s) is not good. Who? ______________________________
   - ❑ Other (please describe): ______________________________

4. **TOUCH/FEEL**: Pay attention to **your reaction to touch or to the things or people you touch/feel** in this setting (check all that apply).

   - ❑ Usually, I do not like others touching me.
   - ❑ Touching things helps me learn.
   - ❑ Things/surfaces feel uncomfortable to touch (sticky, wet, etc.). Please describe them: ______________________________ ______________________________
   - ❑ Sometimes I don't feel pain the way others do.
   - ❑ I have no challenges with the touch or feel of things.
   - ❑ Other (please describe): ______________________________

5. **TASTE**: Pay attention to **tastes or textures on your tongue** in this environment.

   - ❑ I have challenges with the texture or taste of certain foods.
   - ❑ I usually don't put anything in my mouth here.
   - ❑ Other (please describe): ______________________________

6. **MOVEMENT AND SPACE**: Pay attention to **how movement affects you** in this setting.

   - ❑ I cannot sit for long periods of time.
   - ❑ I need to rock, bounce, or press against things.
   - ❑ I have trouble if I need to bend down.
   - ❑ I learn better if I pace or stand up.
   - ❑ I would like to spin in circles.
   - ❑ I have trouble writing on paper.
   - ❑ I easily bump into others or the walls.
   - ❑ I have the right amount of movement or space here.
   - ❑ Other (please describe): ______________________________

7. **OTHER SENSORY INFORMATION**: What other sensory challenges do you experience here? Please describe.

   ______________________________

   ______________________________

Modified from Paradiz, V. (2009). *The Integrated Self-Advocacy ISA™ Curriculum—A Program for Emerging Self-Advocates with Autism Spectrum and Other Conditions.* Lenexa, KS: Autism Asperger Publishing Company (2009). Out of print.

# Chapter 7

## Student Crisis Plan Sheet

Emotional regulation challenges affect up to 80 percent of autistic individuals (Costescu et al. 2021; Mayes et al. 2017), so it is likely that many autistics will experience meltdowns and require instruction and support to develop regulation skills.

Neurological research in autism shows differences in the areas of the brain responsible for regulation (Kryza-Lacombe et al. 2020; Richie et al. 2015). That is, autistics are not automatically able to match emotions and behavior to the environment and change their behavior when a match is not present. Therefore, instruction, supports, coaching, and multiple practice opportunities are needed to ensure that autistics have the skills they need.

Meltdowns occur when the student is exposed to situations they do not have the skills to address. In order to stop the occurrence of these challenging situations, a functional behavior assessment (FBA) is conducted to identify when, where, and why meltdowns occur. A behavior intervention plan (BIP) is then written to detail instruction and supports needed to prevent meltdowns.

### Description

In the same way that the CAPS can be said to be the practical IEP, the Student Crisis Plan Sheet is the practical BIP. By synthesizing information learned about the student in a user-friendly manner, the Student Crisis Plan Sheet helps ensure that everyone on the school team follows the same plan to help the student exert positive control over their environment. It includes the following information:

- A blueprint of events that are likely to precipitate the three meltdown stages: rumbling, rage, and recovery behaviors
- Behaviors the student exhibits at each stage of the meltdown cycle
- Interventions that can be used at each stage to help the student regain behavioral control

- Environmental considerations such as (a) whether others in the environment may need to be relocated and when, (b) who can support the teacher and student during the cycle of meltdowns, and (c) how to document and report the incident. (See Myles 2024 for additional information.)

## Completion of the Student Crisis Plan Sheet

Information from the FBA and BIP is used to complete the Student Crisis Plan Sheet. This "at-a-glance" form summarizes student-specific behaviors and interventions for each stage of the meltdown cycle.

Everyone—classroom teachers, speech-language pathologists, occupational therapists, assistant professionals, paraprofessionals, substitute teachers, and so on—who supports the student should have a copy of the Student Crisis Plan Sheet and receive instruction on how to implement it.

## Summary

The Student Crisis Plan Sheet synthesizes information from the FBA and BIP so that teachers and others are well prepared to support the student who experiences dysregulation. Information from this form can be used to prevent or stop the cycle of meltdowns.

Additional information about the Student Crisis Plan Sheet, the cycle of meltdowns, and how to decrease challenging experiences for the student may be found in *Autism and Difficult Moments: Practical Solutions for Meltdowns* (Myles 2024).

## Student Crisis Plan Sheet

Student Name ______________________________ Student Age/Grade __________

Teacher Name ______________________________ Date of Plan _______________

### ENVIRONMENTAL/PERSONNEL CONSIDERATIONS

1. Describe how you can obtain assistance when it is needed ____________________
________________________________________________________________________
________________________________________________________________________

2. At which stage should outside assistance be sought?

_____ rumbling _____ rage _____ recovery

3. Which school personnel are available to provide assistance?

_____ principal _____ school psychologist _____ paraprofessional
_____ social worker _____ counselor
_____ other (please specify) ______________________________________________
_____ other (please specify) ______________________________________________

4. Where should child(ren) exit to? (specify room or school) ___________________

5. At what stage should the plan be used by others in the classroom?

_____ rumbling _____ rage _____ recovery

6. Are there any extenuating circumstances that others should know about this student (i.e., medications, related medical conditions, home situation)?

7. Who should be notified of the incident? ___________________________________

8. How should the incident be documented? __________________________________

## RUMBLING STAGE

1. What environmental factors/activities or antecedents lead to "rumbling" behaviors?

_____ unplanned change _____ difficult assignment _____ crowds
_____ teacher criticism _____ transitions _____ conflict with classmate
_____ other (please describe) ______________________________

2. What behaviors does the student exhibit during the rumbling stage?

_____ bites nails _____ tenses muscles _____ stares
_____ taunts others _____ refuses to work _____ fidgets
_____ other (please describe) ______________________________
_____ other (please describe) ______________________________

3. Does the student mention any of the following complaints or illness?

_____ stomachache _____ headache _____ not applicable
_____ other (please describe) ______________________________

4. Should the student be sent to the nurse if there is a complaint of illness?

_____ yes _____ no

5. How long does the rumbling stage last before it progresses to the next stage?

______________________________

6. What interventions should be used at this stage?

_____ antiseptic bouncing _____ proximity control _____ touch control
_____ "just walk and don't talk" _____ home base _____ redirecting
_____ other (please specify) ______________________________
______________________________
_____ other (please specify) ______________________________
______________________________

## RAGE STAGE

1. What behaviors does the student exhibit during the rage stage?

_____ student verbally lashes out at teacher
_____ student verbally lashes out at other students
_____ student threatens to hit teacher
_____ student threatens to hit students
_____ student destroys materials
_____ student attempts to leave classroom
_____ student withdraws from teacher
_____ student hurts self
_____ other (please specify) ________________________________
_____ other (please specify) ________________________________

2. What teacher interventions should be used during this stage?

_____ physically move child to safe room
_____ prompt child to move to safe room
_____ remove others from the classroom
_____ redirect student
_____ other (please specify) ________________________________
_____ other (please specify) ________________________________

3. What is the role of others in the child's environment during the rage stage?________
________________________________________________
________________________________________________

## RECOVERY STAGE

1. What behaviors does the student exhibit during the recovery stage without intervention?

_____ sullenness
_____ withdrawal into fantasy
_____ denial
_____ "typical" student behavior
_____ other (please describe) ________________________________
_____ other (please describe) ________________________________

2. What supportive techniques should be used during this stage?________________
________________________________________________
________________________________________________

3. What interventions should be used at a later time to assist the student in gaining more self-control?________________________________
________________________________________________
________________________________________________

## Crisis Report Form

Student Name ______________________________

Teacher Name ______________________________

Setting ______________________ Date ______________

Antecedent Events ______________________________

### Rumbling Stage

Student Behavior ______________________________

______________________________

Teacher Interventions ______________________________

______________________________

### Rage Stage

Student Behavior ______________________________

______________________________

Teacher Interventions ______________________________

______________________________

### Recovery Stage

Student Behavior ______________________________

______________________________

Teacher Interventions ______________________________

______________________________

### Other Considerations

______________________________

______________________________

______________________________

# Chapter 8

## Case Study: Agustin

*This is a true case study. The information provided represents approximately 25 percent of the meetings, correspondence, phone calls, and so on that occurred with regard to this student.*

This chapter is comprised of a comprehensive case study of one young autistic student. Agustin, who friends and family refer to as Gus, has struggled significantly when encountering environments that demanded skills he did not possess. This is the case for many autistic students.

### Fifth Grade

Gus, who is eligible for special education under autism and gifted, attended a general education fifth-grade class with a pull-out gifted class one day a week. The school administrator hand-picked his teachers, selecting teachers whose styles were calm and organized, yet flexible. School personnel received training on autism.

A comprehensive assessment was conducted of Gus at the end of fifth grade. The results revealed the following:

- An intelligence test showed that his IQ was in the very superior range. An achievement test showed that he had above-grade performance.
- The results of an achievement test indicated that he was at or above grade level. Reading comprehension was a strength; mathematical skills and spelling skills were emerging.
- A personality test indicated that Gus easily becomes overwhelmed and may act negatively and impulsively in situations he does not understand. He also exhibited signs of depression and anxiety. Gus is very pessimistic about the future and sees little hope of a positive resolution for his school challenges. He was very concerned about social justice—he often spoke about "fairness."

- A parent-completed behavior rating scale revealed that Gus exhibits the following characteristics:
  - Often fails to pay close attention to details
  - Makes careless mistakes in schoolwork
  - Does not seem to listen when spoken to directly
  - Does not follow through on instructions
  - Fails to finish work
  - Often has difficulties organizing tasks and activities
  - Avoids tasks that require mental effort
  - Loses things necessary for tasks or activities
  - Needs reminders to complete personal care, such as brushing teeth and combing hair
  - Parents further reported that Gus's severe depression may be contributing to his fatigue and irritability.
- A self-report scale indicated that Gus appears to want to conform to teachers' expectations despite teacher reports of oppositional behavior. It is possible that his high level of anxiety and difficulty understanding social cues are underlying factors that create problems in the classroom. Gus views himself as smart but experiences anxiety about his ability to perform academically. Interpersonally, he appears to have difficulty responding to social cues and generalizing rules from one social situation to another. He expresses interest in others but also has sadness and anger about being rejected by his peers at school. He views his parents as providing the nurturance he needs but appears to desire more closeness with them.

Due to his difficulty with adjusting to substitute teachers, his IEP specified that if the general education teacher was absent, Gus would remain with the gifted teacher and provide assistance to younger students in the classroom, and if the gifted teacher was absent, he would remain with the regular education teacher.

Riding the bus was structured for success:

- Assigned seating on the bus with Gus sitting right behind the bus driver
- Gus to sit in a seat alone
- Earbuds used by Gus on the bus

While the classwork in the general education fifth-grade classroom was relatively easy for him, Gus's teachers noted that he (a) experienced difficulty attending to instructions; (b) needed ongoing verbal prompts and help to keep his papers organized; (c) did not turn in homework assignments; (d) had difficulty with writing assignments and long-term projects; (e) engaged in tapping, fidgeting, and making noises; and (f) exhibited challenging behaviors and was suspended twice.

He did not participate in class except to contribute factual information. He often didn't seem to understand creative lessons and said things like, "I still don't understand." Despite not appearing to pay attention to academic work, he can work on an "A" level.

On one assignment, Gus successfully completed the prewriting portion, but then sat in class for twenty minutes doing nothing. This was when Gus's challenges with understanding his environment and the language used by his teachers became apparent. When the teacher asked him why he wasn't doing the work, he answered that his pencil lead had broken. The teacher inquired why he hadn't asked to sharpen his pencil; Gus answered that he didn't think he was allowed to since the teacher had told the class earlier that there was to be "no talking." The school psychologist's observation supported the teacher's notes. A Student Case Management Form revealed a similar problem in misunderstanding that occurred in math class.

| Student Case Management Referral Form | |
|---|---|
| **Student Name:** Agustin | **Date:** 10/28 |
| **Narrative (clearly state why the student is being referred):** During math (9:00 AM), Agustin was making noises and scraping the edge of the desk with his scissors. He was told that he was destroying school property, a serious offense. A few minutes later, he started scraping his pencil with his scissors. When asked why he was destroying the pencil, his reply was, "You said not to destroy school property," in a condescending tone. When this incident was discussed further with Agustin, it became apparent that he thought it was okay to scrape on the pencil because it was his personal property, *not* school property. | |
| **School Staff Signature:** Mr. Terrell | **Role:** Math teacher |

*FIGURE 8.1*

Gus continued to struggle throughout the school year, with similar incidents occurring frequently. He ended the year with passing grades, but he was extremely anxious and depressed.

## Transition Planning for Middle School

In preparation for Gus's upcoming sixth-grade year, the Transition Checklist, Learner Snapshot, IEP, and CAPS were completed in May before the end of fifth grade.

### *Transition Checklist*

Gus's fifth-grade sending team made suggestions for how to support him during sixth grade using the Transition Checklist. A synthesis of Gus's transition needs according to the checklist are summarized here.

- **Environmental supports** include (a) preferential seating, (b) organizational strategies, (c) home base, and (d) a trusted support person. In addition, several personal visual supports were identified. The team also suggested a number of supports that would benefit Gus *and* the rest of his sixth-grade class.

- The following **social supports** are to be integrated into Gus's day: (a) social groups, such as Circle of Friends, Lunch Bunch, and special interest groups; (b) social skills instruction; and (c) social narratives to help Gus understand the routines in each class.

- **Academic supports** include (a) priming to prepare Gus for the school day; (b) assignment modifications that include shortened assignments, task-analyzed assignments, reduced handwriting demands, and models of assignments; (c) no note taking; (d) graphic organizers to provide visual instruction; (e) enrichment; and (f) reduced and modified homework.

- Several **modifications for unstructured and less structured times** were identified in the areas of (a) transitions between classes, (b) bus/transportation, (c) PE, (d) lunch, (e) changing classes, (f) locker, (g) changes in routines, (h) specials, and (i) before and after school.

The fifth-grade sending team suggested that fairly extensive transition planning for middle school begin in May. The parents as well as the members of the sending team (current program specialist, gifted teacher, and behavior specialist) visited several schools to see which program would be the best fit for Gus. These included the neighborhood middle school, a Montessori magnet school, and a science magnet school.

Several of the sending staff felt that Gus might do reasonably well in a program with particularly bright, somewhat nerdy students. In addition, Gus had seen a videotape on magnet programs and had stated interest in attending the science magnet program. Gus met their admissions criteria of scoring in the 75$^{th}$ percentile on an achievement test.

Gus's parents and school personnel met with the coordinator of the magnet program, as well as the exceptional student education specialist from the sixth-grade receiving team, to candidly discuss the kinds of supports Gus might need. Several weeks later, a transition planning meeting was held to plan the transition to the new school. Included in the meeting were the following:

- Representatives from Gus's fifth-grade sending team (elementary school: gifted teacher, behavior specialist, and area program specialist)
- Personnel from the sixth-grade receiving team (middle school: a representative from the district transportation department, a district program specialist, the behavior specialist, the magnet coordinator, the exceptional student education specialist, and inclusion specialists from the magnet program
- Gus's parents

### *Learner Snapshot*

Gus's father completed the Learner Snapshot in May of Gus's fifth-grade year.

**Exceptionality Description:** Autism, gifted

**Family Description:** Gus lives primarily with me and my girlfriend, whom he does not like. Every other weekend, his younger sister, Maria, is here. He spends every other weekend with his mother and sister. The relationship between his mother and me is hostile; however, both are cooperative and involved with his school. Gus's extended family members live out of town.

**Learns Best:** Gus learns best when something is written down or when he is working with his hands. It is extremely important to let him know the schedule at home: mealtime, bedtime, chores, and times he is expected to do things with other family members. I usually write the schedule on a piece of paper and remind him. Gus also needs to know if other people will be visiting, as well as when he will be going to his mother's house and returning.

He loves to read and remembers lots of facts. He also remembers things people have said to him from years ago. He isn't very coordinated and doesn't like physical activities. His handwriting is difficult to read, and he hates having to write a lot. Gus likes to draw, and his drawings are quite good. He can copy a small figure onto a poster board, and the proportions are excellent. He has a very good memory and notices lots of details about places and things.

He has a written checklist of the things he needs to do to get ready on school days. Each task is on a Velcro strip; he removes it and places it in a box after he finishes it. He gets to watch television after he is done. I wake him up two hours before he has to leave for school so he can do all of the items on his checklist and still have TV time. The morning routine does not go well when he is rushed.

**Special Interests/Preferences/Motivators:** Gus likes to read novels as well as factual information on a variety of topics. Over the years, his interests have included dinosaurs, sharks, dolphins, and jellyfish. He likes computer time, movies, and video games. He likes positive interactions with others. He likes to play video games and, sometimes, board games with peers. He likes reading; computer time; praise; high fives; playing a video game or board game with a peer, father, or mother. He also is highly motivated by food.

**Strengths:** Gus does better when he knows his schedule. It is very helpful to write it down instead of just telling him. He likes to know what is going to happen and likes to be ready for each activity. He has a very good long-term memory. He is highly motivated by his favorite interests. When he understands rules, he strictly follows them.

He wants to have friends and does best with those who are serious, do not joke around, and have similar interests. He responds well to praise, especially when he receives it right after he finishes a task.

**Challenges:** Gus has a hard time talking about his feelings—maybe he doesn't know the words. He doesn't seem to know how to make friends. He rarely interacts with peers outside of school. He often over-reacts when there is a change that he is not expecting. He has trouble following verbal instructions and has difficulty solving problems.

He has very poor organizational skills. He tends to hold onto all school papers because he doesn't know what he will need. His backpack is a disaster. He frequently does not turn in assignments or give me notices from school. When he is assigned a school project, he tends to spend way too much time on the first part (like picking the topic) and then is completely behind on the project after that.

**Things That Upset:** Gus becomes very upset when he thinks someone is laughing at him or staring at him. When this happens, he raises his voice and sometimes destroys things or becomes aggressive.

Some smells and sounds bother him a lot. He also overreacts when he is unexpectedly touched. For example, if someone accidentally bumps into him, he thinks they did it on purpose. He doesn't like changes and becomes very anxious when there are any.

If we are going to a friend's house with a lot of people, he needs advance notice. He hates surprises. Unplanned social activities are also troublesome. One day we were in church, and the pastor asked everyone to turn to someone they didn't know and introduce themselves. Gus said, "I don't want to do that." He strongly dislikes when other people (including police officers) break rules and wants to correct everyone, even adults. He seems very uncomfortable when he doesn't know what to do.

**Signs of Being Upset:** When Gus becomes upset, he makes noises and makes faces. Sometimes he throws things. He often refuses to follow directions.

**Effective Ways to Help Your Child Calm Down:** When Gus is upset, it is usually best not to talk too much and to give him space. We usually move away from him. We are working on having him go to his room when he is upset.

**Necessary Supports to Ensure Success at Home, School, and Community:** When Gus gets upset, I tell him to go to his room. I usually say, "Gus, you need to go to your room to calm down." When he goes to his room, he usually goes on the computer. Sometimes he hits his pillow or throws his bedding around.

I always let him know when an activity will begin or end. Usually, I tell him that the activity will begin in fifteen minutes. I do the same when it is five minutes before. We also have a written schedule of activities for the day. Any time we go out (to eat, to Target), I usually plan for him to have down time at home before. He brings things to do in the car when we are going to be out of the house.

### *Comprehensive Autism Planning System*

Gus's fifth-grade sending team did not use a CAPS and appeared reluctant to create one. They provided input on goals and supports for sixth grade. In addition, they suggested that Gus's day begin with priming and that transitions between classes be listed on his schedule.

Gus's sixth-grade receiving team integrated this information into the schedule. The day began with priming that occurred five minutes before students were allowed into hallways:

| | | | | | |
|---|---|---|---|---|---|
| 8:20 | Priming | 11:40 | Transition to Lunch | 2:10 | Transition to Social Skills |
| 8:30 | Computer | 11:45 | Lunch | 2:15 | Social Skills |
| 9:30 | Transition to Math | 12:05 | Transition to PE | 3:15 | Transition to Locker |
| 9:35 | Math | 12:10 | PE | 3:20 | Locker |
| 10:30 | Transition to Language Arts | 1:05 | Transition to World History | 3:25 | Transition to Bus |
| 10:40 | Language Arts | 1:10 | World History | 3:30 | Bus |

Using Gus's schedule, his sixth-grade team, with input from the fifth-grade team, created a CAPS that contained information to support him in priming, lunch, PE, social skills, locker, and bus. A Modified Comprehensive Autism Planning System (M-CAPS) for academic classes and transitions between classrooms was also developed (see figures 8.2 and 8.3, respectively).

| Gus's CAPS for Middle School | | | |
|---|---|---|---|
| Student's name: Agustin | | Date: 5/18 | |
| SS = state standards; I/P = independent/prompted | | | |
| **Time** | **Activity** | **Skills to Teach** | **Structure/ Modifications** |
| 8:20 | Priming (early entry to prime) | • Preparing for the day<br>• Using calming skills<br>• Using a visual schedule | • Visual schedule that indicates when to visit locker<br>• Actual work products |
| 11:45 | Lunch | N/A | • Check in periodically<br>• Assigned table w/ peers |
| 12:05 | PE | State standards | Visual schedule |
| 2:15 | Social Skills | • Scope/ sequence of curricula<br>• Organization<br>• Asking for help | • Visual schedule<br>• Organizational checklists for locker, cleaning out backpack, homework materials needed |
| 3:20 | Locker | • On-time arrival<br>• Gathering materials | • Visual schedule<br>• Map of route<br>• Staff member walks with<br>• Visual in locker of materials needed |
| 3:30 | Bus | Getting on the bus | Assigned seating behind bus driver with a peer |

*FIGURE 8.2*

From *CAPS: Comprehensive Autism Planning System* by Shawn Henry & Brenda Smith Myles, PhD (Future Horizons, Inc. - Arlington, TX - 2024)

| Reinforcement | Sensory/ Regulation | Communication/ Social Skills | Data Collection | Generalization to Community |
|---|---|---|---|---|
| • Verbal<br>• Menu | • Allow to stand, if prefers<br>• Make Another Choice Card<br>• 4-square breathing | Review script asking for help | + participated<br><br>Ø did not participate daily | Visual schedule will be used on the weekends at home |
| Verbal | Home base (self-prompted) | – | – | – |
| • Verbal<br>• Menu | Home base (self-prompted) | Script for asking for help | Gradebook | List of items for school by the front door |
| • Verbal<br>• Menu | – | • Script for asking for help<br>• Conversation starter card | • Scope: Gradebook<br>• Organization: Completed checklist matches materials<br>• Ask for help; need vs. ask/ TR<br>• Help: I/P/T/30 min | List of items for school by the front door |
| Verbal | Movement through the halls | Script for asking for help | – | List of items for school by the front door |
| Verbal | – | – | Y/N on the bus daily | – |

*FIGURE 8.2 continued*

| Gus's M-CAPS for Middle School | | | |
|---|---|---|---|
| Student's name: Agustin | | Date: 5/18 | |
| SS = state standards; I/P = independent/prompted | | | |
| **Activity** | **Skills to Teach** | **Structure/ Modifications** | **Reinforcement** |
| Independent Work | • State standards<br>• Asking for help | • Visual schedule<br>• Assigned seating<br>• ½ problems to complete | • Verbal<br>• Menu |
| Group Work | • State standards<br>• Asking for help | • Visual schedule<br>• Assigned seating | • Verbal<br>• Menu |
| Tests | • State standards<br>• Asking for help | • Visual schedule<br>• Assigned seating | • Verbal<br>• Menu |
| Lectures | • State standards<br>• Asking for help | • Visual schedule<br>• Assigned seating | • Verbal<br>• Menu |
| Transitions Between Classes | • On-time arrival<br>• Gathering materials | • Visual schedule<br>• Map of route<br>• Staff members walks with<br>• Visual in locker of materials needed | Verbal |

*FIGURE 8.3*

| Sensory/ Regulation | Communication/ Social Skills | Data Collection | Generalization to Community |
|---|---|---|---|
| Home base (self-prompted) | Script for asking for help | SS: Gradebook | • Self-prompt for home base at home<br>• List of items to take to school by the front door |
| Home base (self-prompted) | Script for asking for help | | |
| Home base (self-prompted) | Script for asking for help | | |
| Home base (self-prompted) | Script for asking for help | | |
| Movement through the halls | Script for asking for help | | |

*FIGURE 8.3 continued*

### *Middle School Orientation*

In addition to participating in the standard tour of the incoming school with other new magnet students, two weeks prior to the first day of school, Gus went on an individual tour of the school with a representative from exceptional student education. The following briefly summarizes the orientation:

- The tour was videotaped.
- Gus received his schedule.
- Gus walked through the actual schedule.
- Seating was assigned in each class, and Gus tried out assigned seating in each class.
- The bus procedure was explained using a visual.
- The cafeteria procedure was explained using a visual.
- Gus received photographs of each teacher, labeled with teacher's name and subject area.
- School personnel showed Gus completed maps of the school, marking routes from various classrooms to the special education office, as well as to bathrooms from various locations around the school. In addition, when to go to his locker and the route between classes and locker was indicated on the map.
- The procedure for leaving class and going to the bathroom was explained using a visual.
- The home base/break pass procedure was explained and practiced.

### *Staff Training Prior to First Day of School*

The magnet team received a one and one-half hour orientation on autism. All school personnel, including office staff, security, cafeteria workers, etc., were provided information about Gus and home base/break room pass procedure.

# Chapter 8

## Sixth Grade

Gus's educational team and parents felt that the program they had developed would lead to a successful middle school experience for Gus.

### *The First Weeks of School*

In order to help Gus enter school and return home calmly each day, the following was implemented during the first weeks of school:

- Parents dropped Gus off and brought him inside the school for the first few days.
- Support personnel escorted him to each class to monitor transitions.
- Support personnel monitored lunch period.
- Gus was monitored by school personnel before he boarded the bus.

During the first several weeks of school, Gus's parents spoke on numerous occasions to the support personnel to check on how their son was doing. The teachers did not report any problems to support personnel, so they assumed everything was progressing well. But in late September, Gus received an interim report stating that he was significantly behind in some classes. The autism specialist indicated that she thought immediate steps needed to be taken to avoid a crisis. Other school personnel thought that the autism specialist was overreacting. However, several behavioral incidents occurred within the next several weeks that made it apparent to everyone that Gus was having increasing difficulty in several areas. Some of the behavioral incidents follow.

| Student Case Management Referral Form | |
|---|---|
| **Student Name:** Agustin | **Date:** 10/3 |
| **Narrative (clearly state why the student is being referred):** Agustin was at lunch and remarked to the teacher, "It's too noisy in here." I told him he could use his pass if he would like. Failing to do so, within a few minutes, Agustin pounded on the lunch table and walked angrily out of the lunchroom. | |
| **School Staff Signature:** Mr. Gary | **Role:** Lunch monitor |

*FIGURE 8.4*

| Student Case Management Referral Form | |
|---|---|
| **Student Name:** Agustin | **Date:** 10/4 |
| **Narrative (clearly state why the student is being referred):** Agustin refused to move his seat after continued problems with a peer sitting across from him. I gave him a choice to move or I would speak with his dad. When I went to call his dad, he appeared to move, but then he exploded by kicking away his chair and picking up another chair and throwing it across the room and hitting an aquarium. I then suggested that he use his pass; he found it and left. | |
| **School Staff Signature:** Mr. Towerman | **Role:** Science Teacher |

*FIGURE 8.5*

| Student Case Management Referral Form | |
|---|---|
| **Student Name:** Agustin | **Date:** 10/7 |
| **Narrative (clearly state why the student is being referred):** Agustin came into class and slammed his fist on the desk. Threw three textbooks and tore up my teaching materials. Parent contacted: Parent agreed to replace books. | |
| **School Staff Signature:** Mr. Towerman | **Role:** Science Teacher |

*FIGURE 8.6*

By mid-October, the school had assigned an aide to Gus for the entire day. However, the situation did not improve. In a meeting with support personnel, teachers, and Gus's parents, it became clear that the staff had not recognized early signs of stress. For example, Gus exhibited tapping behavior and excessive noise-making in three classes, yet no one intervened or reported the behavior to support personnel. This is problematic in that Gus does not recognize how he is feeling at this time.

### *Traditional Functional Behavior Assessment and Behavior Implementation Plan*

The team decided to meet to review Gus's program and determine how to support him to have a less stressful day. A functional behavior assessment (FBA) was conducted that included observations by school personnel in three academic classes and two less structured periods (lunch and PE). One, conducted in science, is summarized below.

| Student Observation Notes | |
|---|---|
| **Student Name:** Agustin<br>**Class:** Science | **Date:** 10/29<br>**Observer:** Inclusion specialist |
| **Comments:** Agustin did very well and worked the entire class period. He did need to be verbally reminded a couple of times, but when he was reminded, he complied and did his work. Agustin seems to be well prepared in class. I was excited to see him writing down due dates in his planner and was also glad to see him raising his hand to inform his teacher that he was finished with his abstract. His teacher did a great job of checking the dates Agustin wrote down, reminding him to start, and checking on him the one time he showed signs of stress.<br>**Recommendations:** Provide the class with a schedule for the day and remind Agustin when it is time to move on to the next thing. For example, Agustin was reading from his journal and started to write when told to do so. A schedule would help him and his classmates remember to do both as well as a reminder to start writing at a specific time. | |
| **School Staff Signature:** Mrs. Dorfman | |

*FIGURE 8.7*

Each time staff observed Guys' dysregulation, they completed an antecedent-behavior-consequence (ABC) form to assist in developing hypotheses about these behaviors (Sumudre 2020).

His parents were interviewed as a part of the FBA. They described Gus's major behavior challenge as "impulsively reacting in situations where he misunderstands the situation or feels boxed in." In these instances, he may become violent or uncooperative. Gus's parents thought that these behaviors occurred when Gus did not understand what was required of him, misinterpreted the situation, or felt persecuted. The behaviors happened most often when (a) someone made physical contact with him (e.g., brushed up against him in the hallway, bumped him when running in gym)—even if unintentionally; (b) something was taken from him (e.g., such as taking away a distracting Pokémon card, even if warned); (c) he was teased; (d) he was not prepared for changes; (e) his sensory needs were not met; and (f) he did not know what to do. Gus's parents reported that his favorite activities included video games, movies, reading, drawing, and the computer. Further, they reported that he disliked physical activity, writing on topics that were not of interest to him, and working with students he did not like.

The school staff and parents agreed that Gus experienced dysregulation when he was frustrated, interrupted, or surprised. He also had difficulty in social situations, especially when he thought something was unfair or the rules did not make sense to him. They found that Gus exhibited the following behaviors when he was becoming dysregulated:

- Fidgeting
- Head down
- No eye contact
- Rubbing face, head, and hands
- Facial grimaces
- Tearing up assignments
- Rocking in chair

Gus's parents reported that they could usually tell when he was going to lose control by his facial expression. They characterized his expression during this time as angry or tense. In other instances, Gus had made comments about something bothering him, but the amount of distress was not adequately conveyed by his tone of voice or body language. Therefore, they learned to attend carefully to his words. His parents indicated that Gus was often unable to let them know what he needed or wanted. They usually had to listen carefully to his comments or seek more information when they saw signs of stress. Parents and staff also realized that Gus did not recognize that he was distressed until the situation had become a crisis, indicating the importance that teachers react immediately to prevent a meltdown.

Based on the FBA, the team, including the parents, developed a behavior intervention (BIP) that addressed the following issues:

- Gus's behavior is more likely to occur when he shows signs of frustration.
- Gus's behavior is less likely to occur when he is in a highly structured situation, is current on all academic demands, and has positive relationships with those around him.
- Gus's behavior is maintained/reinforced by the ability to reduce/remove stress and anxiety.
- Gus's behavior is reinforced/maintained by escaping or avoiding highly stressful situations.

This information was incorporated into the CAPS and Student Crisis Plan Sheet.

The team then completed the Student Perspective Analysis, the Modified Inventory of Wrongful Activities (MIWA), the Social and Sensory Scan, and the revised IEP. Finally, a new CAPS was developed from the revised IEP.

## *Student Perspective Analysis Summary*

The last week of October, the Student Perspective Analysis interview was completed by the inclusion teacher and Gus. The interviewer was careful to consider times/conditions in which Gus was most willing to answer questions; for example, after meals or snacks or after engaging in a preferred activity. His parents gave him money as an incentive to participate in the interview. Gus was reminded that the information gathered in the interview would help teachers and staff understand some of the things he finds challenging. The following is a summary of information obtained from the Student Perspective Analysis.

**Period I: Computer Class**

- Doesn't understand teacher's feedback
- Has to move away from seat to copy information
- Can't see the board from seat

**Period II: Math**

- Has difficulty copying from board
- Can't read items written in red or yellow
- Is hesitant to speak up because peers may make fun of him
- Is sad about not working with his friend
- Is unclear on how homework is given
- Refuses to write the process in math homework; needs step-by-step breakdown to do so
- Sits near "bugs"

**Period III: Science**

- Doesn't understand teacher's feedback
- Is behind on science project
- Smells of frogs and chemicals are bothersome
- Will not share copy of assignment with parents
- Got an F on the interim test
- Worries about failing class and being kicked out of the magnet program
- Feels air conditioning noises are loud and the room is too cold

- Cannot read teacher notes on the board because they are written in red or yellow
- Problems with two peers calling him names: one, who sits next to him in class, has a whiny, irritating voice; the other kicks him under the table

**Period IV: Language Arts**

- Can't read teacher
- Has difficulty understanding how spelling tests are given
- Has difficulty understanding assignments
- Writing assignments are difficult
- Highly dislikes writing assignments
- Seat keeps being moved by teacher
- Homework is given verbally
- Currently works alone but is given the same amount of work as a group of four. Feels punished for working alone

**Period V: World History**

- Homework given verbally
- Sometimes doesn't hear assignments and fails

Some of Gus's answers may require additional attention. For example, Gus reported that three students bullied him in second hour, third hour, and at lunch. The one student he identified as a friend is not in any of his classrooms. When asked if his third-hour teacher liked him, he replied, "I heard he wants me out of his class. Does that count?"

Although Gus can identify some factors that can make school difficult for him, he does not appear to have self-advocacy skills. He reported experiencing the following issues for which he saw no solution:

- Cannot see the board from his seat in one class; in another class, cannot read teacher notes on the board because they are written in red or yellow
- Sits near bugs in one class
- Is behind on his science project and does not feel he can talk with his dad about it
- May be kicked out of school because he is behind on an assignment
- Sees it as unfair that he has to do the same amount of work as a group of four when he works alone
- Thinks it is unfair that there is very little information available on the mythology character assigned to him to research, unlike the mythology characters assigned to other students

Experiencing problems with no apparent solution causes Gus great frustration. He needs direct instruction, coaching, and multiple practice opportunities on self-advocacy skills and the role of teachers as helpers and problem solvers.

### *Modified Inventory of Wrongful Activities*

The special education coordinator administered the Modified Inventory of Wrongful Activities (MIWA) over several sessions during the last week of October. Gus reported that he had been bullied several times a day in (a) hallways, (b) classrooms, (c) the lunchroom, and (d) by gym lockers. He is not bullied on the bus. He indicated that bullies did the following:

- Pulled his hair, hit, pinched, kicked, tripped, bit, or spat on him
- Said bad things about him and made mean faces at him
- Left him out of a group or activity
- Insulted his ability to learn

Gus also reported that he was afraid to talk in class or make mistakes because he would be teased.

Gus thought some of his teachers didn't like him as much as they liked other students. He further said that he wished his teachers would stop peers from bullying him. At a later point in the inventory, Gus reported that when most of his teachers witness bullying, they "make them stop and teach them not to act that way anymore."

When bullied, Gus said that he generally tells his peers to stop. He said he rarely reports bullying incidents even though this strategy often "helps a lot." When he does report such incidents, he generally talks to his teacher, vice principal, or resource room teacher.

The special education coordinator summarized the inventory by saying that Gus does not have the skills to address bullying and, thus, needs protection and support.

Following completion of the FBA, BIP, Student Perspective Analysis, and MIWA, the school team and parents agreed to revise Gus's IEP. The CAPS and M-CAPS were then also revised. The Student Crisis Plan Sheet was developed based on information from the BIP.

### *The Social and Sensory Scan*

Gus and the inclusion facilitator completed the Social and Sensory Scan for science and lunch because these two environments appeared to create challenges for Gus. He reported challenges in science, consistent with other assessment information, as well as a pronounced mismatch between the lunchroom environment and his needs.

**Summary of Gus's Social and Sensory Scan**

| Item from Scan | Science | Lunch |
|---|---|---|
| **Ratio of Total/ Known People** | 25/3 | 1,000/5 |
| **Adequate Space** | No | No |
| **Visual Directions** | No | No |
| **Expectations Understood** | Yes | Yes |
| **Mood of Others** | Focused | Unknown |
| **Helpfulness of Others** | "I wish the teacher was nicer." | "Nothing is helpful—I hate the cafeteria. I think it might be better not to eat at all." |
| **Sound** | Voices are too loud; may need headphones, unsure | Too many people talking, voices are loud; may need headphones |
| **Smells** | "The frogs and chemicals" | "All of the foods together smell bad" |
| **Touch/Feel** | Prefers not to be touched; dislikes frog skin and anything sticky (glue) | Prefers not to be touched; leftover food on the table feels sticky, gross |
| **Taste** | N/A | Brings lunch from home |
| **Movement and Space** | OK | OK |

*FIGURE 8.8*

### *The Comprehensive Autism Planning System: The Revision*

All information gathered from the (a) FBA, including the observation and BIP, (b) Student Perspective Analysis, (c) Modified Inventory of Wrongful Behavior, and (d) Social and Sensory Scan was compiled. An analysis revealed that it was essential to remove stressors and increase instruction and supports for Gus.

New goals and benchmarks, supports, and data procedures were developed for his IEP and were placed into Gus's new CAPS and M-CAPS. The special educator described the supports Gus needed, and they were created by a paraprofessional. Training on their use was provided to all of Gus's teachers. Photographs were taken of all supports so they could be shared with future teams that supported Gus.

| Comprehensive Autism Planning System (CAPS) | | | |
|---|---|---|---|
| Student's name: Agustin   Date: 11/18   SS = state standards; I/P = independent/prompted; R/R/R = rumbling/rage/recovery | | | |
| **Time** | **Activity** | **Skills to Teach** | **Structure/ Modifications** |
| 8:20 | Priming (early entry to prime 1:1 ratio) | • Asking for help<br>• Using calming skills<br>• Using a visual schedule and mini-schedule<br>• Organizing assignment in notebook<br>• Cleaning out backpack and locker<br>• Class participation<br>• Hall pass procedure<br>• Arrival with materials | • Visual schedule w/change card that indicates when to visit locker, and mini-schedules for each class<br>• Actual work products<br>• Assigned seating<br>• Written procedure for home base practiced multiple times<br>• Social narrative on priming routine |
| 11:45 | Lunch with small group in classroom w/speech-language pathologist | • Scope and sequence of social skills<br>• State standards<br>• Asking for help<br>• Using calming skills<br>• Using a visual schedule and mini schedule<br>• On-time arrival<br>• Arrival with materials | • Assigned table with peers<br>• Social narrative on lunch routine |

*FIGURE 8.9*

From *CAPS: Comprehensive Autism Planning System* by Shawn Henry & Brenda Smith Myles, PhD (Future Horizons, Inc. - Arlington, TX - 2024)

| Reinforcement | Sensory/ Regulation | Communication/ Social Skills | Data Collection | Generalization to Community |
|---|---|---|---|---|
| • Verbal<br>• Menu | • Allow to stand, if prefers<br>• Make Another Choice Card<br>• 4-square breathing<br>• Walking Movement activities (scavenger hunt w/peer)<br>• Hall pass | Review script asking for help | Help: I/P/T/30 min<br>Calm: R/R/R/#/ daily<br>Follow schedule/ mini-schedule: I/P/daily<br>Notebooks: weekly: + satisfactory; 0 help needed<br>Backpack and locker: + satisfactory; 0 help needed/ monthly<br>Participation: +/0<br>Pass: I/P daily<br>Materials: Y/N daily | Visual schedule will be used on the weekends at home |
| • Verbal<br>• Menu | • Home base (teacher/ self-prompted)<br>• Hall pass<br>• Teacher check-in on student mood | • Conversation starter card<br>• Review script asking for help | Initiations/ Responses (compare to peer): #/F/15m<br>SS: Gradebook<br>Help: I/P/T/30 min<br>Calm: R/R/R/#/ daily<br>Home base: Self-/ teacher (S/T) prompted when occurs<br>Arrival: Y/N 1x per week<br>On-time: Y/N daily | Visual schedule will be used on the weekends at home |

*FIGURE 8.9 continued*

From *CAPS: Comprehensive Autism Planning System* by Shawn Henry & Brenda Smith Myles, PhD (Future Horizons, Inc. - Arlington, TX - 2024)

| Comprehensive Autism Planning System (CAPS) *(continued)* | | | |
|---|---|---|---|
| **Time** | **Activity** | **Skills to Teach** | **Structure/ Modifications** |
| 12:10 | PE | • State standards<br>• Using calming skills<br>• Using a visual schedule<br>• and mini schedule<br>• On-time arrival<br>• Arrival with materials | • Visual schedule w/change card<br>• Mini-schedule of activities<br>• ½ time w/class; ½ time in library researching interests<br>• Alternate roles: score-keeper, equipment manager<br>• Teacher-assigned teams<br>• Subtle verbal prompt for on-task<br>• Social narrative on PE routine |
| 3:20 | Locker | • On-time arrival<br>• Gathering materials | • Visual schedule<br>• Map of route<br>• Staff member walks with<br>• Visual in locker of materials needed |
| 3:30 | Bus | Getting on the bus | • Assigned seating behind driver w/peer<br>• Book to read on bus |

*FIGURE 8.9 continued*

From *CAPS: Comprehensive Autism Planning System* by Shawn Henry & Brenda Smith Myles, PhD (Future Horizons, Inc. - Arlington, TX - 2024)

| Reinforcement | Sensory/ Regulation | Communication/ Social Skills | Data Collection | Generalization to Community |
|---|---|---|---|---|
| • Verbal<br>• Menu | • Home base (teacher/ self-prompted)<br>• Hall pass<br>• Teacher check-in on student mood | • Script for asking for help<br>• Use literal and specific words to communicate with student<br>• Group work only when calm<br>• If working individually (not in group), do ¼ problems<br>• Review hidden curriculum item and give example | SS: Gradebook<br>Calm: R/R/R/#/ daily<br>Home base: S/T prompted<br>On-time: Y/N daily<br>Materials: Y/N daily | List of items to take to school by the front door |
| Verbal | • Movement through the halls | Script for asking for help | – | List of items to take to school by the front door |
| Verbal | Noise-canceling headphones, as needed | – | Bus: Y/N/daily | – |

*FIGURE 8.9 continued*

| The Modified Comprehensive Autism Planning System (M-CAPS) | | | |
|---|---|---|---|
| Student's name: Agustin<br>SS = state standards; I/P = independent/prompted | | Date: 11/18 | |
| **Activity** | **Skills to Teach** | **Structure/ Modifications** | **Reinforcement** |
| Independent Work | • State standards<br>• Asking for help<br>• Using calming skills<br>• Using a visual schedule<br>• and mini-schedule<br>• On-time arrival<br>• Arrival with materials | • Visual schedule w/ change card<br>• Mini-schedule of activities<br>• ½ problems to complete<br>• Subtle verbal prompt for on-task<br>• Assigned seating<br>• Teacher check-in on supplies<br>• Use black (not red or yellow) ink to enhance visibility<br>• Prompt to home base daily for practice<br>• Incorporate special interests<br>• Type assignments<br>• Social narrative on class routine<br>• 5-minute prompt to end activity and gather materials | • Verbal<br>• Menu |
| Group Work | • State standards<br>• Asking for help<br>• Using calming skills<br>• Using a visual schedule<br>• and mini-schedule<br>• On-time arrival<br>• Arrival with materials | • Group work only when calm<br>• If working individually (not in group), do ¼ problems<br>• Visual schedule w/ change card<br>• Mini-schedule of activities<br>• Teacher check-in on supplies | • Verbal<br>• Menu |

*FIGURE 8.10*

From *CAPS: Comprehensive Autism Planning System* by Shawn Henry & Brenda Smith Myles, PhD (Future Horizons, Inc. - Arlington, TX - 2024)

<table>
<tr><th>Sensory/ Regulation</th><th>Communication/ Social Skills</th><th>Data Collection</th><th>Generalization to Community</th></tr>
<tr><td>• Home base (self-/ teacher prompted)<br>• Hall pass<br>• Teacher check-in on student mood</td><td>• Script for asking for help<br>• Use literal and specific words to communicate with student</td><td rowspan="2">SS: Gradebook<br>Help: I/P/T/30 min<br>Calm: R/R/R/daily/#<br>Home base: Self-/ teacher (S/T) prompted when occurs<br>Arrival: Y/N 1x per week<br>On-time: Y/N daily<br>Materials: Y/N daily</td><td rowspan="2">• Parent prompt or self-prompt for home base at home<br>• List of items to take to school by the front door</td></tr>
<tr><td>• Home base (self-/ teacher prompted)<br>• Hall pass<br>• Teacher check-in on student mood</td><td>• Script for asking for help<br>• Use literal and specific words to communicate with student</td></tr>
</table>

*FIGURE 8.10 continued*

| The Modified Comprehensive Autism Planning System (M-CAPS) *(continued)* | | | |
|---|---|---|---|
| **Activity** | **Skills to Teach** | **Structure/ Modifications** | **Reinforcement** |
| Group Work *(continued)* | | • Written rules for group work<br>• Subtle verbal prompt for on-task<br>• Assigned seating<br>• Type assignments or someone else writes<br>• Social narrative on class routine | |
| Tests | • State standards<br>• Asking for help<br>• Using calming skills<br>• Using a visual schedule<br>• and mini-schedule<br>• On-time arrival<br>• Arrival with materials | • Visual schedule w/ change card<br>• Mini-schedule of activities<br>• Teacher check-in on supplies<br>• Tests in home base<br>• Study guide for tests<br>• Subtle verbal prompt for on-task<br>• Social narrative on class routine | • Verbal<br>• Menu |
| Lectures | • State standards<br>• Asking for help<br>• Using calming skills<br>• Using a visual schedule<br>• and mini-schedule<br>• On-time arrival<br>• Arrival with materials | • Visual schedule w/ change card<br>• Mini-schedule of activities<br>• Homework is pass-port to class entry<br>• Copy of lecture notes before lecture<br>• Subtle verbal prompt for on-task<br>• Assigned seating<br>• Use black (not red or yellow) ink to enhance visibility<br>• Social narrative on class routine | • Verbal<br>• Menu |

*FIGURE 8.10 continued*

From *CAPS: Comprehensive Autism Planning System* by Shawn Henry & Brenda Smith Myles, PhD (Future Horizons, Inc. - Arlington, TX - 2024)

| Sensory/ Regulation | Communication/ Social Skills | Data Collection | Generalization to Community |
|---|---|---|---|
| | | | |
| • Home base (self-/ teacher prompted)<br>• Hall pass<br>• Teacher check-in on student mood | • Script for asking for help<br>• Use literal and specific words to communicate with student | | |
| • Home base (self-/ teacher prompted)<br>• Hall pass<br>• Teacher check-in on student mood | • Script for asking for help<br>• Use literal and specific words to communicate with student<br>• Review hidden curriculum item and give example | | |

*FIGURE 8.10 continued*

| The Modified Comprehensive Autism Planning System (M-CAPS) *(continued)* | | | |
|---|---|---|---|
| **Activity** | **Skills to Teach** | **Structure/ Modifications** | **Reinforcement** |
| Transitions Between Classes | • On-time arrival<br>• Gathering materials | • Visual schedule w/ change card<br>• Map of route<br>• Visual in locker of materials needed<br>• Early release with peer<br>• All teachers stand outside their classrooms during passing times to observe and support students | Verbal |

*FIGURE 8.10 continued*

| Sensory/ Regulation | Communication/ Social Skills | Data Collection | Generalization to Community |
|---|---|---|---|
| Movement through the halls | Script for asking for help | | |

*FIGURE 8.10 continued*

### *Student Crisis Plan Sheet*

The Student Crisis Plan Sheet was completed to provide specific guidance on how to support Gus when he becomes dysregulated. Emphasis was placed on quickly and calmly responding to Gus's needs.

The team identified the following environmental considerations:

- Trained staff members to provide support during meltdowns, beginning at the rumbling stage
- Peer removal to the atrium with assignment, if needed, and training for peers
- Notification and documentation procedures

In addition, they developed a plan to support Gus if he had a meltdown. Signs of dysregulation, supportive interventions, peer supports, and directions for adults are delineated for each stage of the cycle: rumbling, rage, and recovery.

<table>
<tr><th colspan="3">Gus's Rumbling Stage Information</th></tr>
<tr><th>Antecedents</th><th>Behaviors</th><th>Interventions</th></tr>
<tr><td>Unplanned change</td><td>Angry/tense expression</td><td>Home base with calming items</td></tr>
<tr><td>Difficult assignments</td><td>Rubs body</td><td>Acknowledge difficulties and help</td></tr>
<tr><td>Being bumped</td><td>No eye contact</td><td>Antiseptic bouncing</td></tr>
<tr><td>Something taken away</td><td>Rocks</td><td>Protect student from bullying (if student action); provide warning and reason (if adult action)</td></tr>
<tr><td>Teasing</td><td>Rips assignments</td><td>Protect student from bullying</td></tr>
<tr><td>Doesn't know what to do</td><td colspan="2">Role of Other Students During Rumbling Stage</td></tr>
<tr><td>Unfair situations</td><td colspan="2">Students move to atrium with work (practiced until automatic); assistant principal to supervise</td></tr>
</table>

*FIGURE 8.11*

| Gus's Rumbling Stage Information *(continued)* | | |
|---|---|---|
| **Antecedents** | **Behaviors** | **Interventions** |
| Sensory | **Role of Second Adult** | |
| Interruptions | | |
| Something doesn't make sense | Support other students to move to the atrium and then aid the primary teacher in using needed interventions | |

*FIGURE 8.12*

| Gus's Rage Stage Information | |
|---|---|
| **Behaviors** | **Interventions** |
| Aggression toward others | Home base with calming items |
| **Role of Other Students During Rage Stage** | |
| Students should be in the atrium with work supervised by assistant principal | |
| **Role of Second Adult** | |
| Based on direction from primary teacher (a) relieve assistant principal in atrium or (b) support primary teacher in helping Gus calm. | |

*FIGURE 8.13*

| Gus's Rumbling Stage Information | |
|---|---|
| **Behaviors** | **Interventions** |
| Withdrawal into fantasy | Assignments that Gus can complete independently with ease: review of known information or special interest |
| **Interventions to Teach Needed Skills** | |
| Calming strategies, such as 4-square breathing, interoception curriculum | |

*FIGURE 8.14*

## Summary

During Gus's transition to middle school, the elementary school sending team supplied information using the Transition Checklist and Learner Snapshot. The team did not utilize CAPS and, thus, did not have pictures of past supports to share. The CAPS was created when the receiving team's inclusion specialist interviewed the sending special educator. The sending team believed that the information they shared would create a successful school year for Gus.

Within a short time after the beginning of the school year, Gus's school team, including the parents, realized that the supports that had served Gus in elementary school were not sufficient for middle school. They used the traditional FBA procedure coupled with the completion of the Student Perspective Analysis, Modified Inventory of Wrong Activities, and Social and Sensory Scan to develop a better understanding of the impact of the middle school environment on Gus. This information was compiled into a new CAPS and M-CAPS that provided more comprehensive supports. In addition, the Student Crisis Plan Sheet was created to support Gus in the event he entered the cycle of meltdowns.

The middle school team, including his parents and Gus, felt that the new plan would lead to more success for Gus. They proved to be right.

# Bibliography


Alter, Peter, and Todd Haydon. "Characteristics of Effective Classroom Rules: A Review of the Literature." *Teacher Education and Special Education* 40, no. 2 (2017): 114-127.

Anderson, Melissa, Aliza Werner-Seidler, Catherine King, Aimee Gayed, Samuel B. Harvey, and Bridianne O'Dea. "Mental Health Training Programs for Secondary School Teachers: A Systematic Review." *School Mental Health* 11 (2019): 489-508.

Andrews, J. F., and J.M. Mason. "Strategy Usage Among Deaf and Hard of Hearing Readers." *Exceptional Children* 57 (1991): 536-545.

Arwood, Ellen L., Mabel M. Brown, and Carole Kaulitz. *Pro-social Language: A Way to Think About Behavior.* Oregon: Apricot Inc., 2015.

Begeske, Jasmine, Catharine Lory, Marie David, and Mandy Rispoli. "Teacher Education and Students with Disabilities in Art Class: A Program Evaluation." *Arts Education Policy Review* 124, no. 1 (2023): 48-60.

Bieber, J. *Learning Disabilities and Social Skills with Richard LaVoie: Last One Picked ... First One Picked On.* Washington, DC: Public Broadcasting Service, 1994.

Billeiter, Kenzie B., and John Mark Froiland. "Diversity of Intelligence is the Norm within the Autism Spectrum: Full Scale Intelligence Scores Among Children with ASD." *Child Psychiatry & Human Development* 54, no. 4 (2023): 1094-1101.

Bock, Marjorie A. "SODA Strategy: Enhancing the Social Interaction Skills of Youngsters with Asperger Syndrome." *Intervention in School and Clinic* 36, no. 5 (2001): 272-278.

Bock, Marjorie A. "The Impact of Social-Behavioral Learning Strategy Training on the Social Interaction Skills of Four Students with Asperger Syndrome." *Focus on Autism and Other Developmental Disabilities* 22, no. 2 (2007a): 88-95.

Bock, Marjorie A. "A Social-Behavioral Learning Strategy Intervention for a Child with Asperger Syndrome: Brief Report." *Remedial and Special Education* 28, no. 5 (2007b): 258-265.

Bondy, Andy, and Lori Frost. "The Picture Exchange Communication System." *Behavior Modification* 25, no. 5 (2001): 725-744.

Broupi, Alexandra Eleftheria, Dimitrios Kokaridas, Vasileios Tsimaras, and Panagiotis Varsamis. "The Effect of a Visual Arts and Exercise Program on Communication and Social Skills of Students with Autism Spectrum Disorders." *Advances in Autism* 9, no. 4 (2023): 388-401.

Bruck, Susan, Amanda A. Webster, and Trevor Clark. "Transition Support for Students on the Autism Spectrum: A Multiple Stakeholder Perspective." *Journal of Research in Special Educational Needs* 22, no. 1 (2022): 3-17.

Cannon, Lynn, Courtney Kornblu, Eve Muller, and Michael Powers. *Conversation Club: Teaching Children with Autism Spectrum Disorder and Other Social Cognitive Challenges to Engage in Successful Conversations with Peers*. Lenexa, KS: AAPC Publishing, 2018.

Canon, Jonathan, Amanda M. O'Brien, Lindsay Bungert, and Pawan Sinha. "Prediction in Autism Spectrum Disorder: A Systematic Review of Empirical Evidence." *Autism Research* 14, no. 4 (2021): 604-630.

Carpenter, L. "The Travel Card." In *Asperger Syndrome and Adolescence: Practical Solutions for School Success*, edited by B. S. Myles and D. Adreon, 92-96. AAPC Publishing, 2001.

Cavalli, Gioia, Giovanni Galeoto, Carla Sogos, Anna Berardi, and Marco Tofani. "The Efficacy of Executive Function Interventions in Children with Autism Spectrum Disorder: A Systematic Review and Meta-Analysis." *Expert Review of Neurotherapeutics* 22, no. 1 (2022): 77-84.

Chan, Lynette YL, Teresa Senserrick, and Beth Saggers. "Behind the Wheel: Systematic Review of Factors Associated with Safe School Bus Transportation for Children with Neurodevelopmental Disorders." *Review Journal of Autism and Developmental Disorders* (2022): 1-18.

Clemmensen, Lars, Jens Richardt Møllegaard Jepsen, Jim van Os, Els MA Blijd-Hoogewys, Martin K. Rimvall, Else Marie Olsen, Charlotte U. Rask, Agna A. Bartels-Velthuis, Anne Mette Skovgaard, and Pia Jeppesen. "Are Theory of Mind and Bullying Separately Associated with Later Academic Performance Among Preadolescents?" *British Journal of Educational Psychology* 90, no. 1 (2020): 62-76.

Costescu, Cristina, Mălina Șogor, Serge Thill, and Adrian Roșan. "Emotional Dysregulation in Preschoolers with Autism Spectrum Disorder—A Sample of Romanian Children." *International Journal of Environmental Research and Public Health* 18, no. 20 (2021): 10683.

Danker, Joanne, Shoshana Dreyfus, Iva Strnadová, and Mary Pilkinton. "Scoping Review on Communication Systems Used by Adults with Severe/Profound Intellectual Disability for Functional Communication." *Journal of Applied Research in Intellectual Disabilities* 36, no. 5 (2023): 951-965.

Draper, Ellary A., Laura S. Brown, and Judith A. Jellison. "Identifying Elements of Inclusion: Interviews with Elementary Music Teachers about Their Students with Autism Spectrum Disorder." *Update: Applications of Research in Music Education* (2024): 87551233241237498.

Evans, Martha, and Anti-Bullying Alliance. "Written Evidence Submitted by the Anti-Bullying Alliance." National Children's Bureau, Feb. 2023, committees.parliament.uk/writtenevidence/118262/pdf.

Favreau, Jon, owner Crooked Media. "TikTok vs Biden, Kendrick vs Drake, AI vs Loneliness." *Offline*, season 4, episode 21, May 12, 2024, Accessed May 13, 2024.

Fontil, Laura, Jalisa Gittens, Emily Beaudoin, and Ingrid E. Sladeczek. "Barriers to and Facilitators of Successful Early School Transitions for Children with Autism Spectrum Disorders and Other Developmental Disabilities: A Systematic Review." *Journal of Autism and Developmental Disorders* 50, no. 6 (2020): 1866-1881.

Fujino, Haruo, and Yukiko Ikeda. "Dealing with Food Selectivity and Mealtime Behavior in School-Children with Autism: A Qualitative Study of Special Education Teachers in Japan." *International Journal of Developmental Disabilities* 69, no. 6 (2023): 860-868.

Fusar-Poli, Paolo, Gonzalo Salazar de Pablo, Andrea De Micheli, Dorien H. Nieman, Christoph U. Correll, Lars Vedel Kessing, Andrea Pfennig, et al. "What is Good Mental Health? A Scoping Review." *European Neuropsychopharmacology* 31 (2020): 33-46.

# Bibliography


Gagnon, Elisa. *Power Cards: Using Interests and Enthusiasms to Teach Social Problem Solving and Emotional Regulation Skills to Autistic Students*. Saint Paul, MN: 5 Point Publishing, 2023.

Gara, Sirisha K., Ashok G. Chhetri, Montaser Alrjoob, Sassi Ashraf Ali Abbasi, and Ian H. Rutkofsky. "The Sensory Abnormalities and Neuropsychopathology of Autism and Anxiety." *Cureus* 12, no. 5 (2020).

Gray, Carol. *Comic Strip Conversations™*. Arlington, TX: Future Horizons, 1994.

Gray, Carol. *The New Social Story™ Book, Revised and Expanded 15th Anniversary Edition: Over 150 Social Stories That Teach Everyday Skills to Children and Adults with Autism and Their Peers*. Arlington, TX: Future Horizons, 2016.

He, Jason L., Zachary J. Williams, Ashley Harris, Helen Powell, Roseann Schaaf, Teresa Tavassoli, and Nicolaas AJ Puts. "A Working Taxonomy for Describing the Sensory Differences of Autism." *Molecular Autism* 14, no. 1 (2023): 15.

Heinrichs, Rebekah. *Perfect Targets—Asperger Syndrome and Bullying: Practical Solutions for Surviving the Social World*. Lenexa, KS: AAPC Publishing, 2003.

Heinrichs, Rebekah. *The Modified Inventory of Wrongful Activities*. n.d. Unpublished.

Henry, Shawn A., and Brenda Smith Myles. *Comprehensive Autism Planning System: Implementing Evidence-Based Practices Throughout the Day*. Arlington, TX: Future Horizons, 2024.

Herrero, Jorge Fernández, and Gonzalo Lorenzo. "An Immersive Virtual Reality Educational Intervention on People with Autism Spectrum Disorders (ASD) for the Development of Communication Skills and Problem Solving." *Education and Information Technologies* 25, no. 3 (2020): 1689-1722.

Hwang, Soonjo, Young Shin Kim, Yun-Joo Koh, and Bennett L. Leventhal. "Autism Spectrum Disorder and School Bullying: Who is the Victim? Who is the Perpetrator?" *Journal of Autism and Developmental Disorders* 48 (2018): 225-238.

Hus, Yvette. "Detecting Time Concept Competence in Children with Autism Spectrum and Attention Disorders." *Neuropsychiatric Disease and Treatment* (2022): 2323-2348.

Joli, Nurul Suzaina, Mohd Hasrul Kamarulzaman, Sallehuddin Abdul Rashid, Nursakinah Mat Hazir, Noorsyakina Simin, and Fairuz Adlidna Badrul Hissam. "Curriculum Compacting: Differentiating Statistics Syllabus According to the Readiness Levels of Gifted Students." *International Journal of Education and Pedagogy* 2, no. 4 (2020): 359-367.

Kaplánová, Adriana, Nikola Šišková, Tatiana Grznárová, and Marián Vanderka. "Physical Education and Development of Locomotion and Gross Motor Skills of Children with Autism Spectrum Disorder." *Sustainability* 15, no. 1 (2022): 28.

Koegel, Lynn Kern, Robert L. Koegel, William Frea, and Israel Green-Hopkins. "Priming as a Method of Coordinating Educational Services for Students with Autism." *Language Speech and Hearing Services in the School* 35, no. 3 (2003) 228-235.

Kreibich, Shelley R., Mo Chen, and Joe Reichle. "Teaching a Child with Autism to Request Breaks While Concurrently Increasing Task Engagement." *Language, Speech, and Hearing Services in Schools* 46, no. 3 (2015): 256-265.

Kryza-Lacombe, Maria, Natalia Iturri, Christopher S. Monk, and Jillian Lee Wiggins. "Face Emotion Processing in Pediatric Irritability: Neural Mechanisms in a Sample Enriched for Irritability with Autism Spectrum Disorder." *Journal of the American Academy of Child & Adolescent Psychiatry* 59, no. 12 (2020): 1380-1391.

LaCava, Paul. "Generalization." In *The Comprehensive Autism Planning System: The Comprehensive Autism Planning System: Implementing Evidence-Based Practices Throughout the Day*, edited by Shawn A. Henry and Brenda Smith Myles. Arlington, TX: Future Horizons, 2024.

Lamberti, Emma. "Music Education Within an Autism Support Classroom: Building Community and Educational Skills." *Honors Thesis*. 672 (2024).

Leifler, Emma, Gabriella Carpelan, Anastasiya Zakrevska, Sven Bölte, and Ulf Jonsson. "Does the Learning Environment 'Make the Grade'? A Systematic Review of Accommodations for Children on the Autism Spectrum in Mainstream School." *Scandinavian Journal of Occupational Therapy* 28, no. 8 (2021): 582-597.

Loomis, James W. *Staying in the Game: Providing Social Opportunities for Children and Adolescents with Autism Spectrum Disorders and Other Developmental Disabilities*. Lenexa, KS: AAPC Publishing, 2008.

Mahler, Kelly. *The Interoception Curriculum: A Step-by-Step Guide to Developing Mindful Self-Regulation*. Hershey, PA: Kelly Mahler, 2019.

Mahler, Kelly, Kerri Hample, Carly Ensor, Mary Ludwig, Laura Palanzo-Sholly, Adelaide Stang, Dominic Trevisan, and Claudia Hilton. "An Interoception-Based Intervention for Improving Emotional Regulation in Children in a Special Education Classroom: Feasibility Study." *Occupational Therapy In Health Care* (2024): 1-15.

Martinelli, Katherine, and Dave Anderson. "Why Do Kids Have Trouble with Transitions?" Child Mind Institute. Accessed June 1, 2024. https://childmind.org/article/why-do-kids-have-trouble-with-transitions/#:~:text=Children%20with%20autism%20have%20a,children%20with%20sensory%20processing%20challenges.

Mataya, Kerry, Ruth Aspy, and Hollis Shaffer. *Talk With Me: A Step-by-Step Conversation Framework for Teaching Conversational Balance and Fluency for High-Functioning Individuals with Autism Spectrum Disorder*. Arlington, TX: Future Horizons, 2017.

Mataya, Kerry, and Penny Owens. *Successful Problem-Solving for High-Functioning Students with Autism Spectrum Disorder*. Arlington, TX: Future Horizons, 2012.

Matthews, Michael S., and Julia Hujar. "Using Gifted Education Research in the Classroom." In *Methods and Materials for Teaching the Gifted*, pp. 423-437. London, England: Routledge, 2021.

Mayes, Susan Dickerson, Cari Kokotovich, Christine Mathiowetz, Raman Baweja, Susan L. Calhoun, and James Waxmonsky. "Disruptive Mood Dysregulation Disorder Symptoms by Age in Autism, ADHD, and General Population Samples." *Journal of Mental Health Research in Intellectual Disabilities* 10, no. 4 (2017): 345-359.

McAfee, Jeanette. *Navigating the Social World: A Curriculum for Individuals with Asperger's Syndrome, High Functioning Autism, and Related Disorders*. Arlington, TX: Future Horizons, 2013.

Meilleur, Andrée-Anne S., Patricia Jelenic, and Laurent Mottron. "Prevalence of Clinically and Empirically Defined Talents and Strengths in Autism." *Journal of Autism and Developmental Disorders* 45 (2015): 1354-1367.

Meindl, James N., Diana Delgado, and Laura B. Casey. "Increasing Engagement in Students with Autism in Inclusion Classrooms." *Children and Youth Services Review* 111 (2020): 104854.

Mohamed, Islam Rafaat, and Amira Fawzy Helmy Almaz. "The Role of Architectural and Interior Design in Creating an Autism-Friendly Environment to Promote Sensory-Mitigated Design as One of the Autistic Needs." *International Design Journal* 14, no. 2 (2024): 239-255.

Morton, Hannah E. "Assessment of Bullying in Autism Spectrum Disorder: Systematic Review of Methodologies and Participant Characteristics." *Journal of Autism and Developmental Disorders* 8, no. 4 (2021): 482-497.

Myles, Brenda Smith. *Autism and Difficult Moments: Practical Solutions for Meltdowns.* 25th Anniversary Issue. Arlington, TX: Future Horizons, 2024.

Myles, Brenda Smith, Diane Adreon, and Dena Gitlitz. *Simple Strategies That Work! Helpful Hints for All Educators of Students with Asperger Syndrome, High-Functioning Autism, and Related Disabilities.* Arlington, TX: Future Horizons, 2006.

Myles, Brenda Smith, Elizabeth Grant, and Jocelyn Warren. *Autism and Sensory Issues: Practical Solutions for Making Sense of the World.* Arlington, TX: Future Horizons, 2025.

Myles, Brenda Smith, Melissa L. Trautman, and Ronda L. Schelvan. *The Hidden Curriculum: Practical Solutions for Understanding Unstated Rules in Social Situations.* 20th Anniversary Edition. Arlington, TX: Future Horizons, 2024.

Myles, B. S., Trautman, M. L., and Schelvan, R. L. *The Hidden Curriculum One-a-Day Calendar: Understanding Unstated Rules in Social Situations.* Arlington, TX: Future Horizons. (2025)

Nicpon, Megan Foley, Susan G. Assouline, Pat Schuler, and Edward R. Amend. "Gifted and Talented Students on the Autism Spectrum: Best Practices for Fostering Talent and Accommodating Concerns." In *Special Populations in Gifted Education*, pp. 227-247. New York, NY: Routledge, 2021.

Nuske, Heather Joy, Elizabeth McGhee Hassrick, Briana Bronstein, Lindsay Hauptman, Courtney Aponte, Lynne Levato, Aubyn Stahmer, et al. "Broken Bridges—New School Transitions for Students with Autism Spectrum Disorder: A Systematic Review on Difficulties and Strategies for Success." *Autism* 23, no. 2 (2019): 306-325.

Okada, Naohiro, Noriaki Yahata, Daisuke Koshiyama, Kentaro Morita, Kingo Sawada, Sho Kanata, Shinya Fujikawa, et al. "Longitudinal Trajectories of Anterior Cingulate Glutamate and Subclinical Psychotic Experiences in Early Adolescence: The Impact of Bullying Victimization." *Molecular Psychiatry* (2024): 1-12.

Øzerk, Kamil, Gül Özerk, and Tracey Silveira-Zaldivar. "Developing Social Skills and Social Competence in Children with Autism." *International Electronic Journal of Elementary Education* 13, no. 3 (2021): 341-363.

Panchal, Nirmita, Cynthia Cox, and Robin Rudowitz. "The Landscape of School-Based Mental Health Services." Menlo Park, CA, Kaiser Family Foundation, 2022.

Paradiz, Valerie. *The Integrated Self-Advocacy ISA Curriculum: A Program for Emerging Self-Advocates with Autism Spectrum and Other Conditions.* Lenexa, KS: AAPC Publishing, 2009.

Park, Inhwan, Jared Gong, Gregory L. Lyons, Tomoya Hirota, Michio Takahashi, Bora Kim, Seung-yeon Lee, Young Shin Kim, Jeongsoo Lee, and Bennett L. Leventhal. "Prevalence of and Factors Associated with School

Bullying in Students with Autism Spectrum Disorder: A Cross-Cultural Meta-Analysis." *Yonsei Medical Journal* 61, no. 11 (2020): 909.

Pasqualotto, Angela, Noemi Mazzoni, Arianna Bentenuto, Anna Mule, Francesco Benso, and Paola Venuti. "Effects of Cognitive Training Programs on Executive Function in Children and Adolescents with Autism Spectrum Disorder: A Systematic Review." *Brain Sciences* 11, no. 10 (2021): 1280.

People, Young. "Adolescents Need Play Too: Applying Interventions to Support Social Communication of Girls with Autism in Mainstream Schools." *Children's Research Digest* 5, no. 2 (2018).

Pingale, Vidya, Tina Fletcher, and Catherine Candler. "The Effects of Sensory Diets on Children's Classroom Behaviors." *Journal of Occupational Therapy, Schools, & Early Intervention* 12, no. 2 (2019): 225-238.

Reichow, Brian. "Comic Strip Conversations™." *Encyclopedia of Autism Spectrum Disorders* (2021): 1080-1082.

Richey, J. Anthony, Cara R. Damiano, Antoinette Sabatino, Alison Rittenberg, Chris Petty, Josh Bizzell, James Voyvodic, et al. "Neural Mechanisms of Emotion Regulation in Autism Spectrum Disorder." *Journal of Autism and Developmental Disorders* 45 (2015): 3409-3423.

Roux, Ann. M., Paul T. Shattuck, J. E. Rast, J. A. Rava, and K. Anderson. "National Autism Indicators Report: Transition into Young Adulthood. Life Course Outcomes Research Program," AJ Drexel Autism Institute, Drexel University (2015).

Ruggeri, Anneliese, Alina Dancel, Robert Johnson, and Barbara Sargent. "The Effect of Motor and Physical Activity Intervention on Motor Outcomes of Children with Autism Spectrum Disorder: A Systematic Review." *Autism* 24, no. 3 (2020): 544-568.

Rutherford, Marion, Julie Baxter, Zoe Grayson, Lorna Johnston, and Anne O'Hare. "Visual Supports at Home and in the Community for Individuals with Autism Spectrum Disorders: A Scoping Review." *Autism* 24, no. 2 (2020): 447-469.

Samudre, Mark D., R. Allan Allday, and Justin D. Lane. "Training Preservice General Educators to Collect Accurate Antecedent-Behavior-Consequence Data." *Education and Treatment of Children* (2021): 1-19.

Shelemy, Lucas, Kate Harvey, and Polly Waite. 2019. "Supporting Students' Mental Health in Schools: What Do Teachers Want and Need?" *Emotional and Behavioral Difficulties* 24 (1): 100–116. doi:10.1080/13632752.2019.1582742.

Sheridan, Kayla, Kelly-Ann Allen, Rebecca Vine Foggo, Aida Hurem, Erin Leif, and Nerelie Freeman. "Uncertainty and Autism: How Changing with the Times is Harder for Some." In *Research and Teaching in a Pandemic World: The Challenges of Establishing Academic Identities During Times of Crisis*, pp. 195-212. Singapore: Springer Nature Singapore, 2023.

Stack, Karen, Jennifer E. Symonds, and William Kinsella. "Student and Parent Perspectives of the Transition from Primary to Secondary School for Students with Autism Spectrum Disorder." In *Frontiers in Education*, vol. 5, p. 551574. Frontiers Media SA (2020).

Steiner, Riley J., and Catherine N. Rasberry. "Brief Report: Associations Between In-Person and Electronic Bullying Victimization and Missing School Because of Safety Concerns Among US High School Students." *Journal of Adolescence* 43 (2015): 1-4.

Stickle, Lee, Theresa Earles-Vollrath, and Brenda Smith Myles "Transitions Within and Between Activities: Creating Success for Autistic Learners" (n.d.).

# Bibliography

Swick, Danielle, and Joelle D. Powers. "Increasing Access to Care by Delivering Mental Health Services in Schools: The School-Based Support Program." *School Community Journal* 28, no. 1 (2018): 129-144.

Tamm, Leanne, Amie Duncan, Aaron Vaughn, Rhyanne McDade, Nicole Estell, Allison Birnschein, and Lori Crosby. "Academic Needs in Middle School: Perspectives of Parents and Youth with Autism." *Journal of Autism and Developmental Disorders* 50 (2020): 3126-3139.

Taylor, Kathleen, Kathleen A. Quill, and Marci Laurel. "Communication/Social Skills." In *The Comprehensive Autism Planning System: Implementing Evidence-Based Practices Throughout the Day*, edited by Shawn A. Henry and Brenda Smith Myles. Arlington, TX: Future Horizons, 2024.

TeachThought. "What Are the Best Graphic Organizers for Promoting Critical Thinking?," January 16, 2022. https://www.teachthought.com/critical-thinking/best-graphic-organizers/.

Uherek-Bradecka, Barbara. "Classroom Design for Children with an Autism Spectrum." In *IOP Conference Series: Materials Science and Engineering*, vol. 960, no. 2, p. 022100. IOP Publishing (2020).

Unknown. n.d. "How to Modify Curriculum for Students With ASD." n.d. https://www.crisoregon.org/cms/lib/OR01928264/Centricity/Domain/45/How%20to%20Modify%20Curriculum%20for%20Students%20with%20ASD.pdf.

Vanderbilt Kennedy Center. "Peer-Based Intervention and Autism Spectrum Disorders." April, 2022. https://vkc.vumc.org/assets/files/tipsheets/peerinterventionasdtips.pdf.

Vermeulen, Peter. *Autism and the Predictive Brain: Absolute Thinking in a Relative World*. London, England: Routledge, 2022.

Zepeda, Georgina Solano. *The Vital Role of School Bus Drivers in Supporting Students with Special Needs*. Capstone Projects and Master's Theses. 1756 (2024).

www.ingramcontent.com/pod-product-compliance
Lightning Source LLC
Jackson TN
JSHW061856070625
85404JS00002B/2